W9-BWF-669

785.0924
R56s
119370

DATE DUE			

WITHDRAWN
L. R. COLLEGE LIBRARY

SOLTI

WITHDRAWN
L. R. COLLEGE LIBRARY

SOLTI

Paul Robinson

Discography by Bruce Surtees

CARL A. RUDISILL LIBRARY
LENOIR RHYNE COLLEGE

Vanguard Press, Inc.

785. 0924
R56s
119370
Oct. 1981

The Art of the Conductor
Also available in this series

KARAJAN
STOKOWSKI

Forthcoming

BERNSTEIN
FURTWÄNGLER

Copyright © 1979 by Lester and Orpen Limited.
All rights reserved. No part of this book may be reproduced in any manner whatsoever without permission in writing from the Publishers.

Vanguard Press, Inc.
424 Madison Ave.
New York, N.Y. 10017

ISBN: 0-8149-0802-0

Printed in Canada

Preface

The purpose of each volume in this series, *The Art of the Conductor,* is not to provide a comprehensive biography. Since most of the subjects are (or were at the time of writing) enjoying active careers, this would be a somewhat inappropriate exercise. Rather, my aim is to offer a short reference tool containing the basic facts of a conductor's life to date and a fair assessment of his work in opera and concert and on recordings, based on a cross-section of published opinion as well as on my own observations. The discography at the end of each book is another useful compendium of information about the conductor's work.

In the case of Sir Georg Solti, I have devoted separate chapters to some of the most important phases of his career, including the *Ring* cycle recordings, his years at Covent Garden, and the ongoing and highly successful marriage with the Chicago Symphony Orchestra. There are also chapters dealing with the Beethoven symphony and the Mahler symphony recordings. As these are works which demand special ability and insight, their performance vividly reveals a conductor's powers and limitations. In other chapters I have discussed a variety of operatic and orchestral performances. I have not attempted to say something about every Solti recording, but instead have concentrated only on the most interesting in terms of repertoire or performance.

Like the previous volumes in this series, *Solti* began as a series of radio broadcasts over CJRT-FM in Toronto. Once again I must thank the Station Manager, Cam Finley, and my technician, Ron Hughes, for their help in enabling me to complete that phase of the project. Many thanks also to

Norman Pelligrini, Ray Norstrand, Lois Baum and Tony Judge of WFMT in Chicago, and to the staff of the Chicago Symphony for their help in providing information. A special debt of gratitude to James Creighton of the Recording Archives, University of Toronto, for his valuable advice on the discography.

Introduction

There are many ways of measuring success in the world of music. Good reviews from the New York critics are universally acceptable; so too are high fees. But Solti has long since passed these plateaus. He has enjoyed more special recognition in the form of a knighthood in 1971 and an honorary degree from Oxford the following year. The supreme accolade, however, was awarded him in 1977. That was the year he received a distinction few, if any other, musicians have had conferred upon them: his picture was featured on the cover of the Chicago telephone directory. In all seriousness, it would be hard to discover more conclusive proof of the impact Solti has had on the city of Chicago. During a period in which the Chicago Black Hawks, the Chicago Bears, the Chicago Cubs and the Chicago White Sox have failed to win any kind of glory, the Chicago Symphony has been acclaimed the world over for its greatness.

In recognition and appreciation of the orchestra's international renown, it's members were greeted as conquering heroes when they returned from the 1971 European tour: they were given a parade down State Street and declared "Chicagoans of the Year." The praise has continued to pour in year after year, with ten-minute ovations for the annual New York concerts and showers of awards for the orchestra's recordings. Solti has given the people of Chicago a new and prestigious place in the sun and they love him for it. It is only appropriate that his picture is now in every Chicago home, courtesy of the Illinois Bell Telephone Company.

Who is the man behind this famous face? He is, above all, of course, the conductor of the Chicago Symphony, but that only keeps him in the Windy City for about three months each year. He also maintains a residence in London, where he appears regularly at the Royal Opera House and with the London Philharmonic. A third home for Solti, his wife Valerie and their children is in Italy, where they nearly always spend the summer, completely away from the concert circuit. From September to May, Solti is rehearsing, conducting and recording almost non-stop. During the summer months he insists on setting aside time to reflect and prepare for the following season. He has always been a man in a hurry, although now he more carefully channels his ambition. Instead of one-night or one-week stints all over the world, as in former days, he works mainly with only two orchestras, and for an extended period on each visit. As a result, a mutual respect exists between orchestra and conductor, and neither has to waste time becoming acquainted with the other.

Still, this routine means Solti must jet-travel almost on a commuter basis throughout the year, and he hates it. Those who have travelled with him tell of a man beside himself with fear and anxiety. Yet this is part of Sir Georg Solti: "I have spent my whole life learning to relax," he says. He is incredibly tense onstage and off, and is usually the centre of attention wherever he goes because no one can compete with his dynamism. The infinite number of mundane matters that most people must deal with every day would certainly drive him crazy were he not able to afford to surround himself with a retinue. His wife is Commander-in-Chief, and under her are a secretary, a valet and a housekeeper. When the Soltis take to the road the entourage goes too. Without it the Maestro would be in a permanent state of apoplexy.

What a strange phenomenon! A man at the very pinnacle of a profession which requires that he be in total control of 100 or more men, who is unable to bring any sort of order to the rest of his life without constant assistance. The job of conductor of a major orchestra is comparable in terms of skill, responsibility, pressure, prestige and salary to the presidency of a large corporation. Solti's income from the Chicago Symphony alone would approach a quarter of a million dollars annually. On the other hand, perhaps the anomaly is not so surprising: the demands of the profession are so enormous, a conscientious conductor must give 100 percent to it, and leave the rest of his life for others to hold together.

Solti's anxiety and restlessness were not created by the pressures of the job. He was born with these qualities and to a great extent they make him the kind of conductor he is. Compare Solti with Herbert von Karajan, Conductor-For-Life of the Berlin Philharmonic and often mentioned as Solti's only peer. When Karajan stands on the podium, there is scarcely an unnecessary movement. His feet are stationary; his arms are perpetually extended in a related series of graceful gestures; his eyes are closed and his face is almost immobile. He is not without tension, but it is under complete control. And the sound of the orchestra flows as a consequence. Or, consider Sir Adrian Boult, a former student of Arthur Nikisch and an exponent of his mentor's restrained style. Boult is Karajan with eyes open and without any attempt to choreograph his gestures. Boult is the picture of nonchalance. However, like the great Russian conductor Eugene Mravinsky, this desultory appearance often produces remarkable results.

And then there is Sir Georg Solti:

> Solti is the least graceful conductor since Dimitri Mitropoulos. His motions are jittery; his whole body is in motion; his shoulders as well as his hands are responding to the rhythm; his beat is a series of jabs, and he looks as though he is shadow-boxing. (Harold C. Schonberg, New York *Times*, November 28, 1976)

Solti, it seems, cannot keep still. Even when the music is quiet and slow-moving, he has a tendency to give it a working-over with largely superfluous gestures, so that these more subdued passages emerge with an undercurrent of tension, although sometimes they are simply robbed of repose. Obviously, Solti's elaborate movements are essential to him. They are the only means through which he feels he can adequately express himself, even though so many of them are impossible for an orchestra to interpret literally. One might suspect Solti of trying to impress the audience, except for the fact that his gestures do little to flatter him. And, by and large, they are effective. The players may disagree with what Solti is doing or they might prefer a more straightforward set of signals, but they find him impossible to resist. While Karajan concentrates by going into a sort of trance, Solti's concentration takes the form of total physical involvement, where every part of the body is brought into play. The blazing eyes and the facial expressions — mostly deeply serious and intense, yet also dreamy on occasion — are other vital parts of his technique.

Another aspect of Solti's "everything up front" character is his outspokenness off the concert platform. His remarks to the press about the inadequacies of the Orchestre de Paris caused an almighty row. Nor has he spoken very flatteringly either of the New York Philharmonic, or of tenor Jon Vickers. Even the good burghers of Chicago have felt the lash of his tongue, as when he threatened to do away with the Friday afternoon subscription concerts because the dowagers were so inattentive and noisy in their chatter. Solti is certainly no shrinking violet, but there is a softer side to him too. He is also the maestro who so visibly mellowed after becoming a father late in life, and he is the Hungarian-born musician who was so deeply touched by the honour of a British knighthood for his role in bringing Covent Garden to international standards, that he has preferred ever since to be called "Sir Georg (pronounced George) Solti."

Although his performances rarely display much of a sense of humour, he is capable of entering into the spirit of an event. In his adopted country he has formed a fond affection for former Prime Minister Edward Heath, and on the occasion of Heath's birthday in 1973 Solti made a special contribution to the festivities. At that time, Solti was in

London recording Mozart's opera *Così fan tutte*. He arranged for a recording of the sextet "Alla bella Despinetta" to be played at the party. To everyone's delight the final words had been altered to "Happy Birthday, Ted." The label of this unusual recording read "with harpsichord accompaniment by G. Solti."

In spite of Solti's great love for England, he is still a Hungarian. One of his most recent triumphs was his first concert in Hungary since he fled the country just ahead of the Nazis in 1938. In March of 1978 he returned as part of a tour with the Vienna Philharmonic. It was an unsettling experience for Solti to go back to his homeland, still not free after forty years; to see Budapest, city of his youth; to visit the graves of both parents and a sister. Before he would agree to this trip, Solti stipulated that his fee should be used to enable two young Hungarian conductors to further their studies in the West — a touching personal and political gesture from a man better known for his egocentrism and for his musical achievements.

1
The Making of a Maestro

Hungary is perhaps the world's leading producer of first-class conductors. What other country can boast a list which includes Fritz Reiner, Georg Szell, Eugene Ormandy, Ferenc Fricsay and Georg Solti? Just why this should be so will have to be left to the sociologists. In Solti's case, it was a matter of being blessed with enormous musical gifts and being encouraged to use them.

Solti's father, Mores, grew up in the tiny village of Balatonfokajar, but moved to the capital Budapest to work first in the grain business and later in real estate. Georg, or Gyuri as his family nicknamed him, was born there October 21, 1912. When he was five years old his parents discovered that he had perfect pitch, and although they were far from wealthy they saw the need to develop his natural abilities. They bought an old piano and sent the boy for lessons. Solti took to this new activity with ferocious intensity, quickly demonstrating a precocious talent for the instrument. By the time he was twelve he was giving public recitals.

The following year, Solti enrolled in the Franz Liszt Academy of Music, Hungary's leading music school, for a broader training in music. During his five years there he was fortunate enough to be able to count among his teachers the country's greatest musical figures: Ernst von Dohnányi, Zoltán Kodály and Béla Bartók. It is no wonder, then, that many observers today consider Solti the authoritative living interpreter of the music of these composers.

At some stage during his musical education, Solti was bitten with "the conducting bug." He himself says it happened at age fourteen when he saw Erich Kleiber conduct.

By the time he graduated from the Liszt Academy in 1930, he was positive that conducting was what he wanted to do more than anything else. The problem was, how to begin? Up to this point in his life, he had never conducted.

How does any eager young musician become a conductor? It would appear that the answer, regardless of the difficulties it may present in North America, is to become a coach in an opera house. In fact, nearly all the great conductors were opera coaches at the outset of their careers due to the fact that the job offers practical training. After all, how does a conductor gain experience? He is never allowed in front of an orchestra because he does not know how to conduct. But he cannot conduct because he is unable to practice. Without an orchestra at his constant disposal, he is like a violinist without an instrument. In an opera house, however, the budding conductor acts as a vocal coach, accompanying singers at the piano to prepare them for their roles. He also rehearses the chorus, perhaps even conducting the offstage chorus for performances. After a few years, when he is asked to lead a performance from the pit, he knows inside and out entire operas — not only every note of the score but all the pitfalls. He knows too how to coordinate all the different forces under his command and how to correct mistakes when they occur. He may turn out to be mediocre in his ability to interpret a score or control an orchestra, but at least he comes to the podium prepared.

This is also, by the way, the reason so many of the leading conductors are pianists. If one takes the opera house route to conducting, it is an essential skill. Like Karajan, Szell, Leinsdorf, Klemperer, Walter and so many others, this was the route that Solti followed too. In 1930, at age eighteen, he emerged from the Liszt Academy in Budapest and took his first job in music, as a coach at the Budapest Opera. He was under no illusion that this was a short-cut to fame and glory as a conductor, and it wasn't.

While at Budapest, Solti spent several summers at the

Salzburg Festival serving as an opera coach with Arturo Toscanini. Solti even played the glockenspiel in some Toscanini performances of Mozart's *Magic Flute*. His prowess on this instrument can be examined today on a pirate recording of a 1937 performance. (See discography.) Solti was absolutely spellbound by Toscanini's knowledge, his total dedication, his precision and his drive. It must be said, however, that throughout most of Solti's career he perhaps has been overly influenced by the eminent Italian conductor in matters of both speed and rigidity of tempi. Solti himself admitted as much in a conversation with William Mann in 1974 which was recorded and released as part of the English edition of the Beethoven symphonies.

At Salzburg during the 1930's, Toscanini and Wilhelm Furtwängler were the towering figures among conductors, and altogether different from each other in their methods and interpretations. It must have been extremely difficult for a young conductor to simultaneously appreciate the good qualities of both men. For reasons of prior training and temperament, Solti emulated Toscanini at the expense of Furtwängler, deploring the latter's apparent carelessness in matters of ensemble, tempo and rhythm. As far as Solti was concerned, Furtwängler was completely beyond the pale as a conductor, although Solti later revised this view, recognizing the German maestro's considerable ability after all, and seeking to combine the best of both Furtwängler and Toscanini.

Solti served an eight-year apprenticeship at the Budapest Opera before he got his first opportunity to mount the podium as a maestro.

It was March 11, 1938 and the opera was Mozart's *Marriage of Figaro*. After long years of working, waiting and hoping, Solti was about to prove whether or not he had it in him to be a conductor. If he made a mess of it, he might be denied another chance for years to come, perhaps for good. One can imagine the pressure Solti was under. At twenty-six years of age, determined to be a conductor, impatient that he should have had to wait so long before even beginning, he was at last taking his bows in front of a vast audience and turning to impose his will on orchestra and singers. Would they help him through this terrible initiation or would they delight in showing how green and inexperienced he was?

Unfortunately, it is impossible to report that the young lion emerged triumphant at the end, hailed as "the greatest conductor to appear at the Budapest Opera in the past twenty years." This is the accolade one might expect to find in the biographies of all great conductors, but it is not in Solti's.

For March 11, 1938 was a special day not only for Solti, but for Hungary, Austria and the world. While Solti conducted Mozart's most inspired comic creation, word spread through the house like wildfire that Hitler was only 130 miles away, marching into Vienna. This awful news utterly destroyed concentration both on the stage and in the audience, and Solti's debut became a monumental irrelevancy.

> That was quite a night. All my friends left at intermission. The news came through that Hitler had marched into Vienna, and everybody ran home thinking he was going to continue the march to Budapest. This was a damp ending to my debut. There was not even a celebration after the performance. (New York *Times* interview with Harold C. Schonberg, March 24, 1957)

A Nazi invasion of Hungary was imminent and everyone knew what that could mean for Jews living there. Solti is Jewish and needed no further warning to recognize the need to get out of Hungary. He applied for a visa to go to the United States but was turned down and went to Switzerland instead, where he spent the rest of the war years.

His career as a conductor had already begun late; now it seemed as if it would go no further than an ill-fated debut at the Budapest Opera. From that night it was to be another six years before Solti conducted again. It was only in 1944 that Ernest Ansermet invited him to conduct a few concerts

11

with the Swiss Radio Orchestra. But Solti was by no means idle in Switzerland. Denied the chance to conduct, he poured his energies into the piano, taking occasional engagements as a coach or an accompanist and practising like a demon. In fact, Solti was so gifted and worked so hard he won first prize at a 1942 international piano competition in Geneva.

In the years immediately following the war Solti continued to practise and to perform publicly as a pianist, and most notably as a sonata partner for German violinist Georg Kulenkampf in a memorable series of recordings. Solti's playing in sonatas by Mozart, Beethoven and Brahms is impeccable, and altogether worthy of his, at that time, much more distinguished collaborator. Kulenkampf, nearing the end of his career, was Germany's leading violinist. He died in 1948.

It is commonplace today for conductors to rise to fame overnight. It happens so often that those who do not are dismissed as being demonstrably ungifted. In 1943, at the age of twenty-five, Leonard Bernstein made the front-page of the New York *Times*, stepping in for an ailing Bruno Walter, and emerging victorious. Zubin Mehta was jetting between Montreal and Los Angeles as Music Director of both cities' orchestras before he was thirty. At the same age, Seiji Ozawa was head of the Toronto Symphony and about to take over the San Francisco Symphony on his way to the Boston Symphony within a very few years. Yet Solti, a major talent as things turned out, was not even given a chance to conduct regularly until he was in his mid-thirties.

Had it not been for the war, Solti's career almost certainly would have moved ahead a lot faster. With his talent, he would have become a star of the Budapest Opera and before long, in demand at the more prestigious European opera houses. On the other hand, the war's end unexpectedly benefited Solti. In 1945 there was a dearth of conductors in the German-speaking world. Many of the great ones, such as

Walter, Klemperer, Busch, Szell and Reiner, had fled before the war. Those who had stayed, Furtwängler, Karajan, Böhm and Knappertsbusch among them, were suspected of collaboration and prohibited from conducting until they had been examined by de-nazification tribunals. In the areas of Germany occupied by American forces, Music Control Officers were appointed in an effort to get the opera houses and concert life back to normal. It happened that the officer in charge of the Bavarian section was Edward Kilenyi, an American pianist who had been a classmate of Solti's in Budapest during the 1920's. Either Kilenyi was desperate or Solti had made a remarkable impression on him; whatever the situation, Solti was appointed Music Director of the Munich State Opera.

In normal times such a post would have been out of the question for a man of Solti's inexperience. One of Germany's leading opera houses was not likely to choose as its head a conductor with exactly one opera performance to his credit, and that seven years before! But these were not normal times. In 1945 the Munich State Opera was a pale shadow of its former self. The house had been destroyed by Allied bombing, first-rate singers as well as conductors were in short supply, and there was no money. Music Director Solti lived in one small room in a bombed-out house with no roof.

However, these overwhelming problems were simply minor details in the eyes of the ambitious and energetic Solti. For here at last was the chance to conduct and to conduct regularly—just the learning experience he needed. He developed an enormous repertoire in Munich, including German, Italian and Russian operas and even a number of new works. For example, in the 1949-50 season he conducted *Tobias Wunderlich*, a new opera by Joseph Haas, a pupil of Max Reger's, and in his seventieth year at the time of the premiere. The same season Solti conducted Mussorgsky's *Boris Godounov* in the Rimsky-Korsakov arrangement and orchestration, Verdi's *Rigoletto* with tenor Hans

Hopf as the Duke of Mantua, and Wagner's *Tannhäuser*.

A curious feature of the repertoire of German opera houses at that time was the paucity of Wagner operas. Since Wagner's works had been favoured, even exalted on occasion by the Nazis, their performance was not encouraged by the occupying authorities. Thus, while Solti later became renowned for his Wagner, he was able to conduct very little of it in Munich. *Götterdämmerung* was presented there in 1951 (the first presentation of the work in Germany since the war), but the conductor was Hans Knappertsbusch. The entire *Ring* cycle did not see the light of day in Munich until many years later.

The most prestigious event at the State Opera was always the Munich Festival, in which the Bayerisches Staatsoper put its best productions on show for the international press and public. The English critic William Mann was particularly impressed by a *Salome* he saw there in 1950:

> The most consistently breathtaking of the five Festival performances I saw was without doubt that of *Salome*...Solti's reading brought the clarity of chamber music to this vastly orchestral score, but without losing an iota of the power and polychromatics with which we generally connect it. (*Opera*, 1950)

The following year at the Festival, Solti was again featured in operas by Richard Strauss, leading performances of *Ariadne auf Naxos* with Maria Reining and Wilma Lipp, and *Der Rosenkavalier* with Reining and Sena Jurinac.

It was also in 1951 that Solti was invited for the first time to the Salzburg Festival. This was during a period when the Festival was dominated by Furtwängler who conducted nearly all the operas and many of the concerts himself. Solti was assigned a Mozart opera Furtwängler never cared to conduct: *Idomeneo*. The work is exceedingly difficult to bring off either dramatically or musically. It is written in a more consistently serious style than any of the famous Mozart operas and lacks memorable arias. When one considers that Furtwängler probably appropriated most of the rehearsal time and the best players for his own productions, it is not surprising that one observer had this to say of Solti's performance:

> The orchestral playing was poor. Solti, the conductor, was either fighting a losing battle with tired performers or else not fighting the right battle, and the Italian accents of the singers (apart from Güden) were so execrable as seriously to distort the music. (The Earl of Harewood, *Opera*, November 1951)

It did not help either that Lord Harewood had just seen an extremely successful production of *Idomeneo* at the Glyndebourne Festival. Nonetheless, it was something of a coup for Solti to be invited to Salzburg in the company of many of the leading conductors of the day including, besides Furtwängler, Jochum, Böhm, Stokowski, Kubelik and Edwin Fischer. It must have given Solti great personal satisfaction to return to Salzburg as a full-fledged maestro fourteen years after having served there as a coach with Toscanini.

Solti next appeared at the Festival in 1955, conducting Mozart's *Magic Flute,* a work Furtwängler had always reserved for himself at Salzburg. It was given to Solti only after Furtwängler's death in the fall of 1954. Solti had a fine cast to work with, headed by Elisabeth Grümmer, Erika Köth, Christa Ludwig and Gottlob Frick. The stage director was the highly regarded Gunther Rennert and sets were designed by no less an artist than Oskar Kokoschka. The production received generally good notices, although Solti himself drew some negative comments:

> Musically, the opera received a routine performance. Georg Solti did not seem always to have the orchestra under control and though his tempi were more orthodox than those of his *Don Giovanni,* he did not elicit an unusually distinguished performance. (Christopher Raeburn, *Opera*, October 1955)

On the other hand, when Solti conducted the same work at Frankfurt a few months later, another critic, Andrew Porter, was extravagant in his praise:

> The musical direction of Georg Solti, one of the best of all Mozart conductors, was the triple pillar of the performance: tempi exactly judged, phrasing flexible but firm, and a bewitching balance within the orchestral parts. (*Opera,* December 1955)

The Salzburg invitations were by no means the only ones extended to Solti during his sojourn in Munich. In the summer of 1952 he appeared at the Edinburgh Festival conducting Mozart's *Magic Flute* with the touring Hamburg Opera. And in the early 1950's he made a number of orchestral recordings in London for Decca which did a great deal to make his name known abroad. These recordings with the London Symphony and the London Philharmonic of works by Suppé, Bartók, Kodály and Mozart, set him apart as a conductor of enormous energy and drive, with extraordinary ability to get the best out of an orchestra.

In 1952, after six seasons at the Bayerisches Staatsoper, Solti resigned and accepted a similar post at Frankfurt, where he stayed for a decade. Since Munich was at that time, and still is today, the more prestigious house, it is puzzling that Solti should have made this move. It could be, however, that the decision was not his alone. By 1952, Munich could once more attract the most celebrated names in opera and had perhaps outgrown its need for Solti. Yet even though Frankfurt was not a great leap forward in Solti's career, it did not exactly inhibit his growth either. He continued to expand his repertoire and to mature as a conductor, and his guest conducting elsewhere in the world became more frequent. It was in Frankfurt, moreover, that Solti was noticed by producer John Culshaw and invited to work on the historic *Ring* cycle recording with the Vienna Philharmonic for Decca.

Although Solti did not take over as *General-musikdirektor* until the fall of 1952, his first appearances in Frankfurt were in the spring of that year, conducting Bizet's *Carmen* with Rosl Zapf in the title role. One of the great triumphs of Solti's first season was the premiere performance in Germany of the revised version of Paul Hindemith's opera *Cardillac*, produced by Rennert. It caused a sensation when it was taken to the Berlin Festival in November 1953, earning fulsome praise both for the Frankfurt Opera company and for its new chief:

> It is not considered one of Germany's leading companies and in sheer resources it is clearly inferior to Berlin. But the performances it gave of the new version of *Cardillac* had a unity of style, a sense of musical excitement and a rhythmic vitality that were lacking in most Berlin performances. These qualities were due in the first place to the remarkably fine conducting of Georg Solti. Hindemith's wonderful score is complex — notably in the vast contrapuntal choruses that open and close the work — yet he was clearly the master of every detail, and continued to convey this mastery to his singers and players so that the whole performance shone in what I can only inadequately describe as an intense intellectual and musical luminosity, comparable, perhaps, to the effect the Brahms symphonies made under Toscanini. (Peter Heyworth, *Opera*, November 1953)

Just a month later, however, Solti was involved in a controversial production of Mozart's *Così fan tutte* at Frankfurt. This sublime, eighteenth century comedy of manners was updated to the 1840's, much to the chagrin of many observers, and Solti did not escape unscathed when he decided to conduct the modernized version:

> The efficient, though rather rigid direction of Georg Solti could not redeem this frivolous maltreatment of a masterpiece. (*Opera,* December 1953)

But by 1958, at least one critic had noticed a significant improvement in Solti's conducting of this same opera at Frankfurt:

> His interpretation of *Così fan tutte* in 1958 was characterized as usual by agility, vitality and springy tempos, but whereas his finely balanced sensibility had in the past occasionally lapsed into an overnervy fluctuation of mood and expression, he had now achieved a moment of inner tranquillity which was lacking in his 1954 performances of the same opera. (Ernst Thomas, *Opera*, August 1961)

Yet even in his first years at Frankfurt, there were many who were impressed by Solti's Mozart, particularly his *Don Giovanni*, which was often singled out for praise along with his *Otello*. Both operas seemed to bring out the best in Solti: an almost fanatical attention to rhythmic exactitude coupled with unflagging energy.

> Both performances were conspicuous for their musical discipline which was responsible for the fact, not always to be taken for granted these days, that singers and orchestra were meticulously together. This discipline of Solti's has in it nothing of rigidity. He has the right amount of *Musizierfreudigkeit* to make *Otello* and *Don Giovanni* sound almost as if they were easy to perform. The problematic choral scenes of the first *Otello* act were not only of flawless precision but also completely transparent. The orchestra played very well indeed and eagerly followed Solti's exacting Mozart demands. (Curt Prerauer, *Opera*, April 1953)

Solti also began earning an enviable reputation for his Strauss, Wagner and Verdi. His conducting of *Don Carlos* in 1957 was immensely satisfying to Ruth Uebel:

> Georg Solti certainly belongs to the top rank Verdi conductors of the day. His reading was as exciting as usual, and the brilliant dramatic climaxes never overshadowed those lyrical portions of the score which were lovingly conducted. (*Opera*, December 1957)

And in his review of a new production of *La Forza del Destino* in 1956, Ralf Steyer heaped the highest possible praise on Solti:

> The tender cantabile of Verdi's melody, the dramatic impulse, the vigour of the accents — all this was realized through his understanding of the basic coherence of the drama, in an ideal manner that one knows only from Toscanini and de Sabata. Unfortunately, the stage let him down completely. (*Opera*, December 1956)

But the same critic was quite capable of recognizing Solti's weaknesses, which he thought were particularly glaring in a production of Johann Strauss' *Die Fledermaus* a few months later:

> Solti blew the music away at a jet-propelled tempo so that not merely was the detail not affectionate and clear, but it simply could not be perceived. In addition the orchestra played without delicacy and there were discrepancies on the stage and in the pit...the grand occasion to which we had been looking forward did not come off. It was a pity.

> There was friendly applause, but not the amount that Solti used to receive. (*Opera*, March 1957)

While Frankfurt was not then counted among the leading opera houses in Europe or even in Germany, Solti considerably enhanced its stature both at home and on tour. In addition to the sensational appearance of the company in Berlin in 1953, there was a visit to Paris in 1956 during which Solti conducted Gluck's *Orfeo* and Strauss' *Der Rosenkavalier*, the latter with an excellent cast headed by Maria Reining, Christa Ludwig, Hanny Steffek and Kurt Böhme.

Meanwhile, Solti's personal reputation was growing by leaps and bounds on the international scene. Spring 1953 saw his opera debut in England conducting Mozart's *Don Giovanni* at the prestigious and exclusive Glyndebourne Festival, where he received a favourable critical reaction:

> One enjoyed the drive, virility, and seriousness of purpose which characterized Georg Solti's reading of the score, yet one was less happy about the stage, where with the exception of Jurinac's superb Elvira, and to lesser degree Harshaw's Anna, no one else seemed well cast. (Cecil Smith, *Opera*, September 1954)

Another debut, this time in North America at the San Francisco Opera, took place later that same year. It was one of the most significant events of Solti's career. He conducted both opera and concerts and, moreover, he appeared with the San Francisco Symphony as a candidate for the post of permanent conductor, succeeding Pierre Monteux. Solti conducted the orchestra for three weeks, beginning with a programme comprising Haydn's Symphony No. 103, Strauss' *Don Juan* and Beethoven's Symphony No. 5. He failed to win the post, even though he was well-received by both public and press. His opera conducting in San Francisco was also praised:

> The high point of the German repertory to date was the sensationally tense not to say overwhelming, *Electra,* with Inge Borkh as the heroine, Margarete Klose as an incomparably hag-ridden Klytemnestra, and Georg Solti presiding. Solti is the first guest-conductor to

19

be engaged both by the San Francisco Opera and by the San Francisco Symphony Orchestra and his interpretations of *Electra* and *Tristan* fully justified this innovation. (Afred Frankenstein, *Opera,* December 1953)

An interesting footnote to Solti's North American premiere is that it was not intended to take place in San Francisco at all. He had been invited to conduct the Chicago Symphony at the Ravinia Festival in July of 1953. However, when he applied for a visa at the American consulate in his home base of Frankfurt, it was not forthcoming. The reason given was that Solti's name appeared on a list of members of the "German-Soviet Society," a well-known communist organization in Munich. In 1953 communists were not welcome in the United States. Solti was quick to declare his innocence in a statement issued to the press:

> The list is forged. I testified under oath that I have never been a member of this society, but the consulate officials told me this was not sufficient. The consul believes too that the list is forged, but he said that the matter must be cleared up before I get a visa. (New York *Times*, July 12, 1953)

Solti flew to Munich to get to the bottom of the matter in co-operation with officials of the West German government. Although he was quickly given a clean bill of health by all concerned, his visa was not actually granted until August and he was forced to cancel his Ravinia appearances. Solti's official debut in the United States, therefore, took place September 13, 1953 in San Francisco rather than a month earlier in Chicago.

After San Francisco, Solti began to make annual visits to the United States. His most important engagements were at the Chicago Lyric Opera in 1956. The previous season, Music Director Nicola Rescigno had resigned and the company's financial affairs were in a colossal mess. Miraculously, the chaos was sorted out in time for the next season with an outstanding roster of new conductors, including Solti and Mitropoulos, and the best singers available anywhere, among them Renata Tebaldi, Jussi Björling, Birgit Nilsson and Richard Tucker. Up until this point in his career as an opera conductor, Solti had never had the opportunity to work with such a galaxy of stars and they must have been a large part of the attraction for him in Chicago that season. He conducted Wagner's *Die Walküre* with Nilsson, Paul Schöffler and Christa Ludwig, *Salome* with Inge Borkh, *La Forza del Destino* with Tebaldi, Tucker, Giulietta Simionato and Ettore Bastianini, and *Don Giovanni* with Nicola Rossi-Lemeni as the rake and Leopold Simoneau as Don Ottavio. Solti was consistently criticized for his fast tempos in most of the operas and for tolerating long cuts in *Die Walküre*. His greatest success was with the Verdi:

> This was a performance to be remembered and treasured. Mr. Solti redeemed himself by his judicious choice of tempi and by his ability to keep the huge choral ensembles together. (Howard Talley, *Opera,* January 1957)

The following season Solti was back in Chicago for more Verdi (*Don Carlos* and *Un Ballo in Maschera*, both with Jussi Björling), and Mozart's *Marriage of Figaro*.

Like Solti's North American debut, his long-awaited New York debut did not take place as originally planned. In April of 1957 he was engaged to appear with the Symphony of the Air. This was the remnant of Toscanini's old orchestra, the NBC Symphony, struggling to survive on its own under a new name. It believed, quite rightfully, that it had scored a major public relations coup in presenting a leading conductor's New York debut, and before its arch-rival, the New York Philharmonic. But with the death of Guido Cantelli in a plane crash, the Philharmonic found it had some weeks to fill in the middle of the season. Solti could not ignore the fact that the New York Philharmonic was the better and more prestigious orchestra when he was asked to be Cantelli's replacement for two weeks in March, and he accepted the offer. The Symphony of the Air was furious that Solti's New York debut should be taken from them, and said so to the press. Not surprisingly under the circumstances, Solti's appearance with the Symphony of the Air was cancelled. It seems that the ambitious Solti was not one to allow a good opportunity to pass him by, no matter what prior obligations he might have.

The press coverage for Solti's New York debut could hardly have been more triumphant had he written the reviews himself. Four different critics from the New York *Times* were effusive in their praise. Howard Taubman called Solti's debut "an impressive affair," and remarked that the Hungarian conductor "has a gift of leadership and a mature musical point of view." (March 15, 1957) A few days later, at another concert, a second critic was equally impressed:

> Mr. Solti had made a strong impression at his debut with the Philharmonic on Thursday night. He greatly reinforced that impression yesterday with the drive and intensity of his conducting. He had not got halfway through the Weber Overture [*Oberon*] before it was clear that he was one of those rare musicians to whom there is no such thing as an indifferent phrase. Each note sounded alive with meaning. (E.D., New York *Times,* March 18, 1957)

The following week, Harold C. Schonberg was more restrained but both approving and precise in his remarks. His comments on Solti ring true even after more than twenty years:

> He has very direct notions about music, especially full-blooded music, which is where his inclinations seem to lie. He is not over-subtle, nor does he seek fancy effects. His music-making has a straight, clear line. (New York *Times*, March 22, 1957)

Finally, from a fourth *Times* critic, we have another favourable review, as well as a useful description of Solti's movements on the podium during this period:

> Mr. Solti keeps to a minimum the head-shakings and arm-wavings whereby innocent bystanders suppose conductors to be interpreting the music...His beat was precise but inconspicuous; cues, although infrequent, conveyed the conductor's intentions with graphic vividness. (J.B. March 25, 1957)

For his part Solti praised the New York Philharmonic and his first experience of a great American orchestra:

> The technique is remarkable here. With many European orchestras you have to rehearse many passages to get them just right. Here they know those passages perfectly. And so with very little work you can get the same musical results as with European orchestras, and in addition, you generally have a higher technical standard. (interview with Harold C. Schonberg, New York *Times*, March 24, 1957)

While Solti was involved in the important and concentrated work with the New York Philharmonic — eight concerts during a two-week period with all the attendant rehearsals — it says something for the man's energy that he also managed to attend some plays. He was particularly struck by *My Fair Lady* and *A Long Day's Journey Into Night*.

Solti's career has always been characterized by steady and dogged steps forward rather than by rapid progress. It is not surprising, therefore, that his arrival at the Metropolitan Opera — the absolute summit for opera singers and conductors alike — should not occur until 1960, seven years after his American debut in San Francisco. By 1960, Solti was well-established as Music Director of the Frankfurt Opera, celebrated for his *Ring* cycle recordings on Decca, and known to at least a segment of the American public for his appearances in San Francisco, Chicago and New York. He conducted four performances of Wagner's *Tannhäuser*, at the Met, beginning December 17, 1960 with a cast which included Jerome Hines, Hans Hopf, Leonie Rysanek, and Hermann Prey who was also making his Met debut. At a time when the opera house was being criticized for its dearth of first-rate conductors, Solti's debut was much appreciated:

> Solti's conception of the score, as might be expected, was spacious, imaginative and poignant, and the orchestra under his tutelage was consistently first-rate. (Richard Repass, *Opera*, April 1961)

The pattern of Solti's life in the late 1950's and early 1960's was to spend a few months each year in the United States, several months guest conducting in Europe, and the rest of the time at his home base in Frankfurt. The wonder is that with the increasing demand for his services, he stayed so long in Frankfurt. But he has always preferred to plant roots when he has accepted a permanent appointment. He is a conductor concerned with building and preserving, and he has been highly successful in doing just that in each of his appointments: Munich, Frankfurt, and later, London and Chicago. In 1960, however, the pressure finally became too much and Solti resigned from the Frankfurt Opera to become Music Director of the Royal Opera House, Covent Garden, beginning in the fall of 1961. This appointment signalled the arrival of Georg Solti as one of the most eminent and powerful conductors of the day. Covent Garden was already among the select handful of leading opera houses in the world, and during the ten years of Solti's tenure there, its international stature was enhanced even further.

Solti's farewell production in Frankfurt was Verdi's *Falstaff,* with sets by Caspar Neher and stage direction by Erich Witte. It was lauded as one of the best productions in years with Solti's humorous and poetical conception receiving special praise. His last evening was June 19, 1961. The next day he was in London giving his first press conference as Music Director of Covent Garden.

2
The Maestro Becomes Sir Georg

When Solti was named as the new Music Director of Covent Garden in the spring of 1960, he had also recently accepted the same title with the Los Angeles Philharmonic. Both appointments were announced within a few months of each other and would take effect in the fall of 1961. This meant that for the first time in his career Solti would be simultaneously the head of a major orchestra and a major opera house. The third crucial ingredient in Solti's musical life at this time, albeit a less time-consuming one, was the making of the *Ring* cycle for the first time ever on records. *Das Rheingold* was recorded in 1958, and the other three parts of the *Ring* were completed by late 1965 — a seven-year project that did a great deal to enhance Solti's reputation. It was on the strength of these recordings that critics began to refer to him as "the greatest Wagner conductor alive." Thus, Vienna (for the *Ring* recordings), London and Los Angeles were to be the three points of Solti's compass for the foreseeable future.

Long distance commuting by airplane, an all too common phenomenon today for ambitious conductors, had become normal practice for Georg Solti as early as 1953 when he first visited the United States, and has continued almost unabated ever since. Solti, and others like him, seem to have uncontrollable urges to head up every musical organization they can get their hands on. Perhaps they dare not concentrate on one task lest they botch it and be left with nothing but a bad reputation. Better to keep moving. Or perhaps they are so susceptible to flattery and money they are afraid to turn down offers. Gone are the days when conductors used to remain the entire season with their orchestra or opera house, making only occasional guest appearances elsewhere. Too often in the past twenty-five years, conductors taking appointments continents apart have failed to do justice to any of their obligations and have been doomed, like the Flying Dutchman, to spend their days wandering from city to city, unable to settle anywhere.

Since he left Frankfurt in 1961, Solti has unfortunately fallen into this pattern. Even in Chicago, where his collaboration with the Chicago Symphony has been one of the glories of his career, he spends relatively little time: for example, ten subscription weeks in 1970-71 and eight weeks in 1975-76. What finer orchestra could a conductor want? Yet Solti prefers to spend at least two-thirds of each year elsewhere. With the major orchestras now working fifty-two weeks a year, it is admittedly almost impossible for one man to take charge of all or even the majority of the concerts. Nevertheless, the fact of the matter is that extended absences result in a serious loss of continuity. After his experience as Music Director of the Boston Symphony, Erich Leinsdorf suggested that what was needed was a permanent musical administrator instead of a permanent conductor. The manager of an orchestra generally does not deal with purely musical matters; but a music administrator could do so without waiting for the return of the maestro. In any case, this is a serious problem for which a solution must be found if orchestras and opera companies are to develop as ensembles with their own style and personality.

As things turned out, Solti did not get a chance to test the viability of his Los Angeles connection. Before his first season had begun, a crisis erupted which forced his resignation. It seems that the President of the board, Mrs. Norman B. Chandler, had taken it upon herself to appoint Zubin Mehta as the orchestra's Assistant Conductor while Solti was away. Solti immediately objected on the grounds that such matters were the sole perogative of the Music Director. He asked for assurances that no further similar actions would be taken and that Mehta be given seven weeks as Guest Conductor over the next two seasons and not eight as arranged by Mrs. Chandler. When no such assurances were forthcoming, Solti cancelled his April 1961 appearances with the orchestra and resigned as Music Director. This meant an instant promotion for Mehta who was appointed as Solti's replacement. Solti insists that he had nothing against Mehta in the dispute; he simply could not tolerate the affront to his artistic authority:

> I was in London, and it was sent to me by cable saying "I hope you agree to that." [The "that" was the appointment of Zubin Mehta as Assistant.] I said "no." And that was the end; because Mrs. Chandler had to save her face and I must save mine. The musical director has to make decisions. When a decision is made over his head, he must put a stop immediately. It was not a question of personality—this assistant conductor or that one—it was a question of principle. So I resigned—before I ever started. (*High Fidelity*, October 1969)

Unfortunately, the elimination of Los Angeles from Solti's life did not free up any of his time for the Royal Opera House. He simply filled in the gaps in his schedule with guest conducting stints elsewhere. In 1962 he even took on the musical direction of another American orchestra. Unlike his experience with the Los Angeles Philharmonic, Solti actually got to conduct some concerts with the Dallas Symphony but the "marriage" lasted only one season. During the course of his ten seasons at Covent Garden he conducted no more than twenty-seven performances in a single season (1969-70), sometimes as few as twenty (1963-64 and 1968-69) and only fifteen in his last season. In fairness, it must be pointed out that Colin Davis, Solti's successor at Covent Garden, averages about the same number of performances. Again, it is the problem of tying a conductor down to one job.

Solti had first appeared at Covent Garden in December 1959, conducting *Der Rosenkavalier*. He had been warmly praised:

Georg Solti made a welcome Covent Garden debut and drew some
magnificent playing from the orchestra. There were some wonderful
sonorities, rather lacking in recent Strauss performances here, and
some very sensuous playing. What one missed was tenderness—but
that was a quality lacking in the performance as a whole, except when
the divine Jurinac was on stage. (Harold Rosenthal, *Opera,* January
1960)

So it followed that when Rafael Kubelik resigned as Music
Director of Covent Gardens, Solti, one of the first-rate opera
conductors available at that time as well as one who had
already made a good impression in the house, was offered
the job by Lord Drogheda, Chairman of the Royal Opera
board. Solti declined at first saying that he had had enough
opera for the time being. He was about to resign his post in
Frankfurt and go to Los Angeles. However Sir David
Webster, Covent Garden's Managing Director, pursued
Solti to Luxembourg for further negotiations. By then, Solti
was more interested, but before making up his mind he
asked the advice of Bruno Walter. When Walter advised
him to accept, Solti gave in and signed a three-year contract.

Solti made his next appearance in the pit at Covent
Garden early in 1961 directing a recently composed British
opera, Benjamin Britten's *A Midsummer Night's Dream.* At
this point, Solti had been announced as the new Music
Director, although he did not take charge until the fall of
that year. But it was a shrewd move to have him direct a
British opera in a house becoming increasingly sensitive to
the question of foreign domination of repertoire, artists and
conductors. The board of Covent Garden made it very clear
to Solti that British composers must be encouraged and that
British performers were to be used wherever possible.

At his first press conference in June of 1961, Solti was
reassuring on all counts as he laid out his plans for future
seasons. He announced that he intended to make the house
"the best in the world." Further, he promised to use and
develop British artists and said that he was planning a
revival of Britten's *Billy Budd* as well as new productions of

Tippett's *King Priam* and Walton's *Troilus and Cressida*. He was in favour of performing certain operas—comic, Slavic and modern works—in English rather than in the original language. In terms of non-British repertoire he specifically mentioned operas such as Schönberg's *Erwartung* and *Moses und Aron*. The completion of both a Mozart cycle and a *Ring* cycle was also in his plans. And Solti was obviously not merely dreaming. During the course of his ten-year regime at Covent Garden only two operas on his original list—*Faust* and *Lulu*—were not performed.

The first new production in the Solti era was an offbeat choice: Gluck's *Iphigénie en Tauride*, a rarely performed opera, well out of the mainstream. Solti conducted performances at the Edinburgh Festival in the fall of 1961, then brought the production to London where it received mixed reviews. A more important assignment came a few weeks later when Solti entered the pit to conduct his first Wagner at Covent Garden: *Die Walküre*. On the strength of his recorded *Ring* cycle, as yet only partially completed but nonetheless widely acclaimed, and his work in Munich and Frankfurt, Solti was already highly regarded as a Wagner conductor, and much was expected of this new *Die Walküre*. The producer was the experienced and admired Wagnerian bass Hans Hotter who also sang Wotan in the production. His contribution, as it happened, was traditional and often dull. The sets by Herbert Kern were even less impressive; in fact, reaction was so negative that Kern was dismissed and another designer engaged to take over the rest of the *Ring* cycle. So it was left to Solti and the singers to carry the day. With a cast featuring Jon Vickers, Hotter, Rita Gorr and a solid group of British singers including Claire Watson and Michael Langdon—and the splendid Josephine Veasey among the Valkyries—there was little to fault, and Solti himself won plaudits for the intensity and drive of his conception, and for the wonderful playing of the orchestra. At least musically, it was an auspicious beginning for the new *Ring* cycle.

On a less positive note, this series of *Die Walküre* performances turned out to be the last collaboration between Vickers and Solti at Covent Garden. Such was the tension that developed between them at rehearsals that Vickers refused to sing henceforth in any productions conducted by Solti. The Canadian tenor thought that Solti bullied him. For his part, the conductor complained that Vickers was unco-operative, and said as much in a letter to Vickers:

> I feel I must say first of all that I am very disappointed with our collaboration in *Walküre* especially as I felt that your co-operation was somewhat lacking. I regret this very much because I feel strongly that each individual vocal part must fit into the whole scheme in order to make a homogeneous performance...I felt that I met with a rejection of almost every suggestion. (*The Quiet Showman*, M. Haltrecht, 1975)

Solti and Covent Garden had hoped to have Vickers for *La Forza del Destino* and *Otello* in the near future, but Vickers would agree to sing only if Solti were not in the pit. Solti himself took the initiative in trying to lure Vickers back, particularly for the revival of *Die Walküre* as part of the complete *Ring* cycle in 1964; still the tenor could not be persuaded. Solti's *Ring* cycle would have to proceed without the greatest Siegmund of the day. Vickers has never again sung with Solti, and the conflict between the two was one of Solti's greatest frustrations during his tenure at Covent Garden.

Later in his first season, Solti was in charge of an unusual triple bill produced by Peter Ustinov, which included Schönberg's *Erwartung*, Ravel's *L'Heure Espagnole* and Puccini's *Gianni Schicchi*:

> In all three there were the hallmarks we have come to recognize in all Solti performances: excitement, tension, beautiful orchestral tone, and the revelation of details in the score hitherto unheard. (Harold Rosenthal, *Opera*, August 1962)

At the end of the 1961-62 season, critics were generally pleased with what Solti had achieved, and were inclined to be tolerant where there was room for improvement. But in the second season the gloves were off. Even Solti's Wagner was no longer regarded as sacrosanct. In fact, the editor of *Opera*, Harold Rosenthal, began a persistent series of attacks on Solti's Wagner which continued throughout the conductor's tenure as Music Director. Reviewing the 1962 *Siegfried*, Rosenthal began the assault:

> It is also inclined to be loud, and thrilled as I was to hear great surges of orchestral sound, I felt a trifle battered by the beginning of Act 3. What I did find missing was tenderness and poetry. (October 1962)

But the unmitigated disaster of Solti's second season was without doubt a new production of Verdi's *La Forza del Destino*. The trouble began when producer, Sam Wanamaker, quarreled with the designer, Guttoso. Guttoso quit and Wanamaker ended up designing the sets himself, but not to the satisfaction of Sir David Webster who thought them too sparse for grand opera. Wanamaker also chose to stage the work *à la* Brecht at the expense of Verdi's intentions, and to the absolute bewilderment of the singers. Carlo Bergonzi, an outstanding Italian tenor but never much of an actor, was the leading man, and his female counterpart was not the scheduled Leontyne Price but the vocally insecure Floriana Cavalli. The results have been vividly recalled by Montague Haltrecht:

> At the first night the duel scene had elements rather of Chaplin than of Brecht, Bergonzi first losing his sword, and then suffering further embarrassment when his visor dropped...Cavalli sang disastrously flat and more or less without voice. The huge aria of the final act was awaited with dread, and as the poor thread of a voice uncertainly emitted an approximation of the last notes, another voice from the gallery, hissed out, charged with venom — "This is disgusting! Where's Shuard?" The unfortunate Cavalli came before the curtain at the end of the evening, and as her body bent in a bow it seemed as though she was being broken by the weight of booing. (*The Quiet Showman*)

In his last appearances of the season, conducting Mozart's

31

Marriage of Figaro, Solti fared no better, being accused by the *Times* of "skating over the score." Unfortunately, by the end of this nightmare of a season Solti's contract was up for renewal, and there was no question as to what his decision would be. He had been persuaded to come to Covent Garden in the first place only after much hesitation, and now, with all the abuse from the press, Solti's first inclination was simply to get out while the going was good. He had never before encountered such criticism in his career and it hurt him. But Sir David Webster and the board of the Royal Opera had become strong believers in Solti and did everything they could to persuade him to stay. Solti is a stubborn man and eventually he resolved to dig in his heels and carry on. This decision also had much to do with the fact that Solti had never conducted a complete *Ring* cycle in the opera house, and it mattered to him that he remain long enough to do so.

In his third season Solti conducted the postponed *Billy Budd* and *Götterdämmerung*, the final part of the *Ring*, although the complete cycle would not be given until the following season. With *Billy Budd*, Solti scored a major personal triumph, demonstrating once again his affinity for the music of Britten:

> Georg Solti's handling of the score was one of his best achievements. Sometimes he pressed the music forward too urgently: the most serious case in point was at the F major chordal arch, which had almost intolerable vividness in Britten's own graver yet more sharply coloured handling. But he seemed to catch all the score's flying brilliance and mighty groundswell, and steered his elaborate forces with a certain hand. (John Warrack, *Opera*, March 1964)

Although not British by birth, the Music Director of Covent Garden had championed the country's leading opera composer, just as his successor Colin Davis would do for Michael Tippett. Solti's belief in Britten helped to affirm that operas by living British composers were welcome at Covent Garden, even if the repertoire was otherwise rather reactionary in character. When Britten died in 1976, Solti spoke of him with affection and added a personal recollection of their work together on *Billy Budd*:

> I felt that the *piano* marking for an *espressivo* passage did not give enough sound, so I asked Ben if it could be changed to *forte*. We played it through changing the *piano* to *forte*—"I like it," he said. "Lets keep the Solti version." But in the end I was sorry I had made the suggestion as I truly preferred the original *piano* marking! He was always most encouraging and at the same time highly critical but in a constructive rather than negative sense. I adored working with him.
>
> Britten was an operatic genius. His departure has left an enormous emptiness in the world of music and in the lives of his friends. (*Opera*, February 1977)

Solti's biggest success that season, however, was not with Britten or Wagner, but with Verdi. Harold Rosenthal went out of his way to praise Solti's conducting of *Otello*:

> I am quite convinced that this *Otello* is the finest thing Solti has so far done at Covent Garden. This is *his* opera beyond any doubt, and I wonder if there is a finer *Otello* conductor anywhere in the world? Solti combines the nervousness of a Beecham with the burning incandescence of a de Sabata, to which he added his own special gifts of virility and the ability to judge and calculate orchestral sonorities. One would perhaps welcome a little more expansiveness, especially over the more lyrical moments of the score. (*Opera*, June 1964)

But when Solti's eagerly awaited *Ring* cycle appeared the following autumn, Rosenthal was even more annoyed by Solti's Wagner than he had been by the conductor's *Siegfried* two years before:

> I wish I could have seen a musical and dramatic shape in it...Mr. Solti's climaxes do not seem to be related one to the other, and themes, leading-motives, call them what you will—are often played in quite different ways...the Forest Murmurs was almost devoid of poetry...the Rhine Journey was far too fast...and the noise of the Funeral March was almost vulgar. (*Opera*, November 1967)

John Greenhalgh, writing in *Music and Musicians*, was equally critical:

> They [brilliant orchestral sound and exciting climaxes] are no compensations for failing to sustain the whole work, despite its length.

Under Solti the music of the *Ring* has been more a series of fragmented episodes, as he has moved from one climax to another, the threatening *longueur* in Wagner's music thereby kept at bay. (March 1971)

In spite of this strongly negative reaction to Solti's *Ring* from some observers, the production of the entire work was a major achievement for Covent Garden. And with Solti's recorded cycle nearing completion to a crescendo of favourable comment, it was a coup for this opera house that such a celebrated Wagner conductor should do his first *Ring* with them.

If the new Solti *Ring* drew a mixed reaction in the 1964-65 season, so too did *Moses und Aron* on an even grander scale. The work is so difficult to play and sing and the problems for the producer so complex, that it had been staged only twice before, in Zurich and Berlin. Solti was one of the instigators of the project for Covent Garden, even though he was advised by friends not to do it; they said it was impossible. Yet Solti regards the work as magnificent and went ahead anyway. The producer was Peter Hall, Managing Director of the Royal Shakespeare Company but a new face at the Royal Opera House. His wry comment was: "Any director likes to be challenged by the impossible."

There are those who dismiss *Moses und Aron* for its dissonant, tuneless score, and call it a scenic oratorio because of its biblical text and its lack of action. Schönberg wrote the libretto himself and often his stage directions seem meant for some "opera house of the mind," as Peter Hall put it, rather than for anything as temporal as the Royal Opera House, Covent Garden. Here is an example from a scene in Act 2:

The priests embrace and kiss the maidens. Behind each pair a girl stands with a long knife and a jug for catching the blood in her hands—the girls hand the priests the knives. The priests seize the virgins' throats and thrust the knives into their hearts. (Scene 3)

The opera deals with the problem of finding faith and of communicating religion to the masses without corrupting the message. The most spectacular scene in the work and the one which attracted the most attention in the press following the London performances was "The Golden Calf and the Altar," an orgy on a lavish scale. In previous productions little attempt had been made to depict the debauchery on stage, but Hall insisted on making the scene as realistic as possible: "If you do the orgy stylized I don't think the horror would be unleased." (BBC interview) To achieve his purpose, Hall covered the entire stage with naked couples in the act of copulation. Audience reaction ranged from "shocking" and "vulgar" to "boring," but the customers came. All performances were sold out, with scalpers getting as much as twenty-five guineas a ticket. Apart from the orgy, the audience was treated to a spectacle involving a chorus of 130, forty-five actors, twenty children, fifteen dancers, thirty extras, and a veritable zoo which included six goats, a bullock, a horse and two donkeys and, in Peter Hall's words, "a very large orchestra spattered in blood [from the activity on stage] in the pit."

Seven weeks of intensive rehearsals went into the production, and the hard work paid off. Solti and Hall received most of the praise; Solti for making the abrasive score as clear and as exciting as it could possibly be, and Hall for his extraordinary conception. Hall's participation was undeniably crucial to the entire project and helped erase memories of *La Forza del Destino*. Particularly unforgettable were his richly detailed crowd scenes. But *Moses und Aron* was very much a team effort which did a great deal for Covent Garden's prestige. The opera house had demonstrated that it could attract some of the best talent in the country and be innovative on a very high level.

Solti's faith in the score of *Moses und Aron* led him to conduct it at the Paris Opera and with the Chicago Symphony in a concert version. Unfortunately, while Solti must be the most experienced *Moses und Aron* conductor alive, he has not recorded the opera because the costs for a work involving so many performers would be astronomical.

The same season which saw the production of *Moses und Aron* and an entire *Ring* cycle also contained Solti's first Covent Garden performances of a Richard Strauss opera. The work he chose was *Arabella*, which he had recorded in Vienna a few years before. Here again production standards were very high, with Rudolf Hartmann directing and Peter Rice designing the sets. The cast was headed by Dietrich Fischer-Dieskau and Lisa Della Casa. With Solti in the pit, it was the *Arabella* of a lifetime for those who saw it.

The following season (1965-66) Solti repeated his *Ring* cycle and *Moses und Aron*, added another Wagner opera—the *Flying Dutchman*, revived *Der Rosenkavalier* which had brought him such success at his Covent Garden debut, and continued the projected Mozart cycle with the *Magic Flute*. It was his fifth season as Music Director and he was now comfortable in the role. He was respected for his recent achievements with Wagner, Strauss and Schönberg, and, in fact, there was a general feeling emerging that Solti was one of the best things ever to happen to Covent Garden. The London house could now boast more performances of a consistently high standard musically, dramatically and visually, than its opposite numbers in Milan, Vienna, Munich and New York. Even the troubled Harold Rosenthal admitted that perhaps Solti had achieved the goal he had set himself at his first press conference: to make Covent Garden "the best opera house in the world." But in a conversation with the conductor in 1968, Rosenthal pursued one of his favourite themes—that Covent Garden was still not doing enough to develop British artists. Solti's answer was the same as it had been in 1964 when Rosenthal had first brought up the topic:

Covent Garden is an international house, and we are not really the training ground for young artists—they grow up and develop at Sadler's Wells and with Scottish and Welsh Opera for the most part. (*Opera*, June 1968)

At the height of his popularity at Covent Garden, Solti made a firm and publicly announced decision to leave at the end of his tenth season, 1970-71. It was time, he said, to set opera aside for a while and to conduct more concerts:

> I will have spent ten years here — a nice round period — and twenty-five or so years in opera. It's time for a change. I want to catch up on my concert career. But of course I will not give up conducting opera and I hope I'll be invited back to Covent Garden. (*Opera*, June 1968)

In his last years at Covent Garden there were more triumphs in store for Solti, particularly with Strauss—*Die Frau ohne Schatten* and *Salome*—and with Wagner—*Tristan und Isolde* (this last marking his farewell appearances as Music Director in the spring of 1971.) Jess Thomas sang Tristan with Birgit Nilsson and Ludmila Dvoráková alternating as Isolde. The producer was Peter Hall. The collaboration of conductor and producer recalled the success of *Moses und Aron* a few seasons back in raising standards on the stage and in the pit to a uniformly high level:

> If there is a real major achievement in the production it is that Peter Hall has imposed a consistent acting style, to a greater extent than I have ever seen, on a largely established cast, and on international principals...such beautiful playing Solti drew from the orchestra that one was transported...sad goodbye to a Wagner conductor who really has reached maturity and greatness. (Tom Sutcliffe, *Opera*, August 1971)

Even so, Harold Rosenthal expressed his usual reservations about Solti as a Wagner conductor:

> Solti is never at his best on first nights, and as so often in the past, I was rather disappointed in him as a Wagner conductor. The *Prelude*, taken very slowly, almost fell apart, and each act seemed to be treated as a separate entity with its own scale of dynamics, rather than as part of a whole...at the last night things went much better. (*Opera*, August 1971)

The night of his final performance, all manner of tributes were paid to Solti including a KBE presented by Prime

Minister Edward Heath, a great music-lover and sometime conductor himself. Solti was knighted by Queen Elizabeth shortly after he became a British citizen about a year later. He was enormously proud of his acceptance by the British people and chose henceforth to be called *Sir* Georg Solti.

During his ten years at Covent Garden, Solti had also become more British in the sense that he had divorced his first wife Hedi, whom he had met in Switzerland during the war, and married Valerie Pitts, a young reporter sent to interview him for the BBC-TV. The affair began in 1964, and after both parties had obtained divorces they were married in 1966. According to people who know the couple well, Valerie is responsible for transforming Solti from an arrogant and sometimes tempestuous maestro into a more relaxed and domesticated figure. Certainly his conducting did show signs of mellowing during the 1960's and Solti was seen to be spending much of his time with his newborn first child, Gabrielle.

Summing up Solti's ten years at Covent Garden, Harold Rosenthal gave him credit for tremendous improvement in the general standard of performance in the house, and for bringing "his own brand of electrical excitement into the theatre — a kind of glamour, which only existed on limited occasions previously." (*Opera,* October 1971) But the critic took strong exception to Solti's own assessment of what he had done:

> When I arrived in London there was a beautifully kept semi-amateur opera house. Now it is fully professional. (Interview with John Higgins, *Times,* June 12, 1971)

This comment, in Rosenthal's view, exhibited a remarkable ignorance of the many exceptionally enjoyable evenings in the pre-Solti era, presided over by the likes of Kleiber, Beecham, Giulini, Kempe, Kubelik, etc., none of them noted for their "semi-amateur" affiliations.

Rosenthal also very much lamented Solti's failure to

develop the nucleus of a true ensemble in the house, using British singers. But in Solti's defense it must be said that there is today not a single major opera house in the world operating with such a system. What was possible in the European opera house of the twenties and thirties was out of the question by the sixties. Costs were too high and audiences all too aware of the world's great voices on records; they insisted on hearing the stars and not the unknown local artists. No major opera house today could pay the bills with the sort of rep group that stayed together from opera to opera in the old days. Rosenthal castigated Solti for achieving only a series of "fine, festival-like productions with hand-picked casts," (*Opera*, October 1971) when no music director anywhere could have done more.

Rosenthal wanted to see more British singers in leading roles, more new British operas, and more British producers and designers working in the house. But when one considers that these are matters for which Solti was not solely responsible, his efforts on behalf of British nationalism were considerable under the circumstances. British singers of the stature of Gwyneth Jones, Peter Glossop and David Ward were used whenever possible; three Britten operas and two by Tippett were mounted as well as Walton's *Troilus and Cressida*, Bennett's *Victory* and Searle's *Hamlet*. This is by no means a radical record, but it is well above the average in the ranks of major opera houses. Covent Garden, moreover, is no place for trying out the first efforts of unknown composers. There should be other less costly venues for that.

As for producers, Solti was successful in attracting Peter Hall to work on *Moses und Aron, Tristan und Isolde,* and the *Knot Garden*, and excellent work was also done by Visconti, Zeffirelli, Copley, Kaslik and Hartmann.

Since his retirement as Music Director in 1971, Solti has returned regularly to Covent Garden to conduct major new productions including *Electra* (October 1972), *Carmen*

(October 1973), and *Die Frau ohne Schatten* (June 1975, repeated April 1976). However, he did leave Covent Garden to resume his *concert* career, and with few exceptions that is exactly what he has done, mainly in Chicago but also in London. The year he left Covent Garden, he took up a new appointment as conductor of the Chicago Symphony and began what many regard as the most important phase of his career.

3
The Maestro at the Summit

The Chicago Symphony has a proud and illustrious history. It was founded in 1891 by Theodore Thomas, one of the most dynamic and influential conductors of any age. It is also due to Thomas that Orchestra Hall was built in 1904 especially to house the Chicago Symphony, the first auditorium in the United States ever constructed for the exclusive use of a symphony orchestra. When Thomas died in 1905 he was succeeded by Frederick Stock, who had been Associate Conductor under Thomas. During Stock's thirty-eight year tenure the Chicago Symphony gained world renown, especially through its recordings, the first of which were made in New York in 1916. On the orchestra's fiftieth birthday, in 1941, major composers, Stravinsky, Milhaud, Kodály, Glière, Harris and Walton among them, were commissioned to write works for the occasion.

Stock was followed in fairly rapid succession by Désiré Defauw (1943-47), Artur Rodzinski (1947-48) and Rafael Kubelik (1950-53). Fritz Reiner began his ten-year sojourn as Music Director in 1953 and under his direction the orchestra became famous for its virtuosity and discipline (most notably in works by Richard Strauss, Wagner and Bartók), and for its quality of sound which many observers felt combined the best of European and American orchestras.

The Reiner era ended with the conductor's death in 1963. He was succeeded by Jean Martinon, about whom argument continues to this day in Chicago. In some quarters Martinon is praised as a fine musician with particular expertise in contemporary music, who expanded the orchestra's repertoire. But others think he was pedantic in his treatment of

41

the orchestra and out of his depth in much of the bread-and-butter repertoire, i.e., German music, which the orchestra had learned to play so well under Reiner.

Martinon's ultimate downfall was caused by his failure to get along with too large a segment of the orchestra. The bad feeling which developed between the pro- and anti-Martinon factions of the orchestra continued long after his departure from his post in Chicago (in 1968) and even after his departure from this world (in 1976).

The principal thorn in Martinon's side was the long-time and universally-respected principal oboist Ray Still. He so disliked Martinon's behaviour as man and conductor, and so often argued with him during rehearsals, that Martinon decided the troublesome oboist would have to go if he were to maintain his authority as Music Director. Unfortunately for Martinon, Still dug in his heels and fought the firing through the orchestra, the union and the courts. In the end, after a great deal of bitterness, Still won his case to stay on with the Symphony and Martinon was finished. Of the many players who took Martinon's side in the dispute, one was principal flautist Donald Peck. Still has neither forgiven Peck nor even spoken to him since, even though they sit beside each other day in and day out. When Solti took over he was apprized of the situation and tried to act as mediator for the two players, but Still refused to budge. Solti himself, who has been involved in very few arguments with the orchestra, had a run-in as well with Still. Solti described what happened:

> At a recording, a very good wind was displeased with the way he had played, and he stopped to redo it. However, I did not want to stop, knowing quite well the merits of what we were doing, and that eventually a small incident could be edited out. But he did not continue to play his part. Thus, I was forced to stop the performance, and I made a small scandal. This has been the only time in five years, where I have had to remind one that the decision to play or stop was mine only. (*Harmonie,* September 1974)

Ray Still is obviously a very difficult man but he is also one of the glories of the Chicago Symphony and the recording studio incident notwithstanding, he and Solti have developed a relationship of mutual respect.

With Martinon on his way out, the Orchestral Association of the Chicago Symphony set about to find a suitable replacement. The key figures involved in the search process were Louis Sudler, the Chairman, and John Edwards, the Executive Vice-President and General Manager. Sudler was a highly accomplished singer who had been active in the Chicago Civic Opera productions of the 1940's. When his vocal career came to a standstill he threw himself into his real estate business and emerged with a very large fortune. He joined the board of the Chicago Symphony in 1964 and became President two years later. It was a bad time for the orchestra. In addition to the Martinon crisis, huge deficits were piling up and there did not seem to be much that could be done to rectify the situation. Moreover, the renovation of Orchestra Hall to provide better amenities for the players and the audience had succeeded in destroying the hall's much-praised acoustic excellence. Needless to say, none of this did much for orchestra's morale or its fund-raising efforts. The future looked very grim indeed for the new President.

One of Sudler's initial priorities was to find a first-class manager for the orchestra — a man with the vast experience of orchestra management necessary to restore stability and help plan for the future. Through luck or persuasion, Sudler found the ideal person in John Edwards. Here was a man who had worked for half the orchestras in the United States, and who knew the musical world like the back of his hand. With over thirty years' experience behind him, Edwards was one of the most gifted and imaginative planners and problem-solvers around. At the time he was approached by Sudler, Edwards was quite contentedly managing the Pittsburg Symphony. He had already turned down the Chicago job once before, in 1964. The second time around, however, flattered at receiving so much attention from one of the "Big Five" orchestras and excited by the chance to be in on the choice of a new conductor, he accepted the offer.

Sudler had decided that the Chicago Symphony was a great orchestra and deserved the finest conductor in the world. He believed, quite rightly, that if the musical end of things were healthy, corporations would be more inclined to contribute. The choice he and Edwards settled on was Herbert von Karajan, the most famous conductor alive and also the most expensive. The problem was that he was Conductor-for-Life of the Berlin Philharmonic and almost totally disinterested in even guest conducting American orchestras let alone taking a permanent post with one of them. Two weeks with the New York Philharmonic in 1957 had been enough, thank you very much. It was unrealistic of Sudler and Edwards to think they could lure Karajan to Chicago but it is a measure of their ambition and determination that they chased the Austrian maestro all over Europe seeking his acceptance. When it became obvious that Karajan's indifference to the job was genuine, they began to seriously consider other conductors and to think about the real possibility that more than one man might be necessary for the job. With the orchestra now on a year-round schedule and star conductors unwilling to restrict themselves to one orchestra, there was a good chance that the Chicago Symphony might be unable to find the single conductor it wanted.

After Karajan, the most celebrated conductor at work in 1967 was Solti. His *Ring* cycle recordings had made him a star and the standard of performance he had achieved at Covent Garden was the talk of the musical world. In fact, the Chicago Symphony had approached Solti before Martinon in 1963, but Solti had declined the offer because it would have demanded too much of his time. Two years into Covent Garden this was an understandable response. But five years later Solti was feeling the need for a change, especially one that would allow him to spend more time on concert work and less on opera. However, as much as he wanted the Chicago post, he also wanted to leave himself relatively free for guest conducting in Europe. By this time, the new management of the orchestra had come to accept the fact that it could not expect more of a conductor of Solti's stature, and the two parties reached an agreement. Solti would assume his position in Chicago in the fall of 1969 conducting only about ten weeks each season plus several weeks of touring. The orchestra was to institute regular visits to New York, and make its first-ever European tour in the very near future.

The initial approach to Solti by Sudler and Edwards had involved a breathtaking and ingenious scheme that would have seen Karajan as Music Director with Solti and Carlo Maria Giulini as Associates or Principal Guest Conductors. In the light of their temperamental and musical differences, one can scarcely imagine Karajan and Solti sharing the same orchestra, but what an exciting triumvirate that would have been!

Still, the actual outcome of Sudler and Edward's negotiations was not unimpressive. Giulini readily agreed to serve as Principal Guest Conductor with Solti as Music Director. Giulini is not an ambitious man and was happy to leave the administrative end of leading an orchestra to Solti (although to nearly everyone's surprise he has since accepted the post of Music Director of the Los Angeles Philharmonic). For his part, Solti went out of his way to accommodate himself to Giulini with respect to choice of repertoire. Unfortunately, the plan broke down after a few seasons, with Giulini gradually withdrawing into the role of Occasional rather than Principal Guest Conductor. He remained long enough, however, to win the love of the orchestra and a vast and adoring audience in Chicago. It was not until the coming of Henry Mazer in 1970 as Associate Conductor that the orchestra attained a much-needed measure of stability at last.

Solti was not unfamiliar to Chicago audiences. He had conducted the Chicago Symphony in 1954 at the Ravinia Festival in a programme which included Tchaikovsky's Symphony No. 5, and had worked with the Lyric Opera during the 1950's. In December of 1965 he had appeared for the first time at Orchestra Hall. When he took over in Chicago in 1969 he was still the Music Director of the Royal Opera House, Covent Garden. Following his departure from Covent Garden two years later, many people thought he was intending to expand his activities in Chicago. By 1971 he had already had a considerable impact on the orchestra and after the Chicago Symphony's first European tour in the fall of that year, audiences and press alike were ecstatic in their praise of the remarkable chemistry between Solti and the great American orchestra. This was Solti's first full-time orchestral appointment and it had very quickly added a new dimension to his reputation. But to nearly everyone's consternation, Solti did not increase his commitment to Chicago by a single week, nor has he done so since. Instead, he took on new posts with other orchestras: first, the Orchestre de Paris and then the London Philharmonic.

Solti's involvement with the French orchestra was a short-lived and stormy affair which ended disastrously in 1975 largely because, as he himself admits, he did not give the job enough of his time. Since Solti's task in Paris was to raise a second-class orchestra to the top rank, one wonders why, with a first-class orchestra in Chicago already clamouring for more of his time, he would be interested in trying. The same question could have been put to Herbert von Karajan when he took on the Orchestre de Paris before Solti, while continuing as chief of the Berlin Philharmonic. Nor are Solti and Karajan exceptional in this regard. Perhaps the most extreme example of this multi-directorship occurred when Seiji Ozawa, not content with the Boston Symphony, decided to head up orchestras in San Francisco and Tokyo at the same time.

But why do so many conductors today feel the need to

take on more than one orchestra at a time? More specifically, why does Solti do it? For Solti the reasons are both personal and professional. On the personal side, he dislikes Chicago and has from the beginning. His remarks to the press about the city's lack of cultural sophistication have gotten him into hot water on several occasions. In particular, he has been outspoken about the dreariness and inattentiveness of subscription audiences, especially the Friday afternoon dowager crowd: "I don't believe in one-sex audiences." After nearly a decade in Chicago, Solti and his family still behave as visitors instead of residents. Their current pattern is to fly in for each semi-annual six-week stint and to fly out immediately afterwards. Home in Chicago is the Drake Hotel. But in fairness, Solti has appeared at civic functions and on WFMT-Radio during the station's yearly fund-raising marathon for the orchestra (the total raised during a single weekend in 1978 was $400,000). His wife Valerie has also participated in the activities of the orchestra. She has taken part in several of the Petite Promenades given for Second and Third Grade students, including a *Carnival of the Animals* and a puppet version of Humperdinck's opera *Hänsel und Gretel* for which she provided the narration.

Solti's fondness for England also has much to do with his absences from Chicago. In fact, the Soltis' winter season home is really London. Solti's success at Covent Garden, the "thank you" he received in the form of a knighthood and, above all, his English-born wife combine to draw him back to the city. Nearly every season he conducts at Covent Garden and directs concerts and recordings with the London Philharmonic. When he was recently offered the principal conductorship of the orchestra, it came as no surprise that he accepted the post.

In addition to the English connection, Solti maintains his long-standing practice of devoting his summers to private study at his home in the Italian village of Roccamare, 125 miles north of Rome. Each summer, while the Chicago

Symphony is grinding out three concerts a week at Ravinia north of Chicago, Solti is recharging his batteries at his Tuscan retreat. This means that almost alone among the Music Directors of major American orchestras—Maazel and the Cleveland Orchestra at Blossom, Ozawa and the Boston Symphony at Tanglewood, Ormandy and the Philadelphia Orchestra at Robin Hood Dell and Saratoga—Solti does not lead his orchestra in any concerts during its summer season. It should be pointed out, however, that the administration of the Ravinia Festival is quite independent of the Chicago Symphony. The orchestra is simply hired to be in residence there. Ravinia also has its own Music Director, currently James Levine, who has nothing whatever to do with the orchestra's winter season. But Solti has no wish to conduct at the festival anyway. The limited rehearsal time, the poor acoustics, the noise of the audience would all drive him crazy.

Solti's professional motivations for limiting the number of weeks he wishes to spend in Chicago are even more compelling. He argues that the amount of time he gives to the Chicago Symphony is about right for the artistic well-being of both himself and the orchestra. To remain longer in Chicago would be to risk the fruitfulness of the relationship for both parties. There is little to fault in this reasoning. Even the most loving marriage partners need some time away from each other. An ill-prepared Solti, a Solti bored or irritable after facing the same orchestra for too many weeks at a stretch or, on the other hand, an orchestra suffering from too much exposure to the same conductor might very well turn out lacklustre performances. Solti is an extremely tense and demanding conductor, capable, over short stretches, of producing a high level of concentration and excitement in the orchestra. However, this kind of tension can only be maintained for a limited period, then it must be replaced by a more relaxed atmosphere. The Solti-Giulini combination provided just this kind of dichotomy. The two conductors are equally serious but Giulini is a much quieter man, more concerned with line and poetry than with power and precision.

Solti's actual annual commitment to the orchestra is no less than that of other eminent maestros. The most highly regarded conductor and orchestra combination in Europe, Herbert von Karajan and the Berlin Philharmonic, record at a ferocious pace, tour extensively and, in general, seem to be inseparable. Yet Karajan conducts the orchestra for approximately only fifty concerts each season. Solti's seasonal total in Chicago is about the same. He conducts roughly one-quarter of the concerts given by the orchestra over a twelve-month period. During the 1977-78 season he was in Chicago for four weeks in the fall and back for seven weeks in the spring. In addition, there were some tour concerts, most importantly, the annual visit to New York, and a number of recording sessions. The 1978-79 schedule comprises ten weeks of subscription concerts in Chicago preceded by a four-week European tour. The remaining weeks in the orchestra's season are filled by Henry Mazer, the Associate Conductor, who is in charge of most of the youth concerts; James Levine, who conducts most of the Ravinia programmes (twelve in 1978); and numerous guest conductors.

Twelve to fifteen weeks may not seem like a lot of time for a music director to devote to an important orchestra. With so many open weeks in the orchestra's schedule, surely standards must decline during the director's long absences. In fact, this is not the case with the Chicago Symphony. Because Solti is expected to present a different programme each season and not to repeat any given work more than, say, once every three or four years, he must always be adding to his repertoire, something which requires a fair amount of his time. However, since the Chicago Symphony is among the foremost orchestras of the world, excellent guest conductors are not difficult to find, and Solti has had little problem persuading some of the best to commit themselves to annual appearances.

In the 1977-78 season, for example, in addition to Margaret Hillis, Director of the Chicago Symphony Chorus, who conducts one subscription concert every season, there were five guest conductors: Carlo Maria Giulini, Daniel Barenboim, Erich Leinsdorf, Gennady Rozhdestvensky and Leonard Slatkin. Giulini has continued his association with the orchestra and has appeared for an extended period in nearly every season. The other four are returning as guests in 1979-80. Each is currently in great demand but has chosen to commit himself to the Chicago Symphony. This provides an extremely valuable element of continuity in the orchestra's activities, while in no way jeopardizing standards. The other conductors for 1979-80, by the way, include such eminent maestros as Claudio Abbado, chief conductor of the Vienna Philharmonic and La Scala, and Carlos Kleiber in his North American debut. When Solti is away Chicago audiences may miss him, but they are certainly not having to put up with inferior conductors in his place. At the same time the orchestra is being exposed to a cross-section of the best leadership that can be found.

It should also be kept in mind that the music director of an orchestra of the Chicago Symphony's calibre must excel in everything he does. If he allows himself to be overextended in terms of preparation or repertoire, performances will suffer, and recordings or one of his guest conductors will make this all too obvious. Even the greatest conductors do not conduct everything equally well and they must try to recognize their own limitations. With a well-chosen roster of guest conductors, a wider repertoire can be covered for the benefit of the audience, and the music director can be free to present himself in what he does best.

In Solti's case, the necessity for taking time out to learn new repertoire is compounded by the considerable pressure on music directors of American orchestras to programme music by native composers. For a foreign-born conductor like Solti, this has meant learning a good deal of music that, otherwise, he might not be inclined to touch. He has been criticized for playing too little American music in Chicago, but his record is not bad. Each season he has personally conducted two or three works, often world premieres. In 1970-71, for example, he premiered Levy's *Piano Concerto* and Alan Stout's *Symphony*. The following season he conducted Elliott Carter's *Variations for Orchestra*, Charles Ives' *Holidays* Symphony, and the *Cello Concerto* by Miklos Rozsa. At the same time Solti has regularly programmed new or difficult scores by non-American composers. In recent years he has given first performances of *Heliogabalus* by Hans Werner Henze and the Symphony No. 4 by Sir Michael Tippett. And how many conductors of American orchestras have ever put on Arnold Schönberg's notoriously complex opera *Moses und Aron?* Solti conducted it in Chicago in 1971 and then took it to New York shortly afterwards. Solti may be identified with the Bruckner-Mahler-Strauss repertoire, but one cannot deny that he has done excellent work in other areas too, not least of all in twentieth-century music.

When Solti agreed to come to Chicago for the fall of 1969, one of his conditions was that the orchestra expand its touring. It was an expensive proviso but Solti thought it was a necessary investment to raise the Chicago Symphony's profile. If New York and Europe could hear the orchestra they would surely be impressed, and glowing reviews and tumultuous ovations would improve both playing and fund-raising efforts. The orchestra had been to New York before, under both Reiner and Martinon, and in 1959, during the Reiner era, a European tour had been scheduled but then cancelled at the last moment due to the conductor's illness. It was not until Solti took over the orchestra that it had the opportunity to travel extensively. In 1971, Solti and the Chicago Symphony presented twenty-five concerts in fifteen cities, including London, Berlin, and Vienna. They were received with almost boundless enthusiasm. European audiences and critics had heard fine American orchestras before—Chicago was the last of the Big Five to cross the ocean—but after so many good reports, so many distinguished recordings, and above all after such a long wait, it must have been a special thrill to see and hear the Chicago Symphony. In 1971, at the end of its second year, it was one of the most fortuitous conductor-orchestra marriages of modern times.

Three years later the orchestra returned to Europe to even greater acclaim, except in Paris. Solti was, at that time, also head of the Orchestre de Paris and had made some rather harsh comments about the orchestra's ability. He brought the Chicago Symphony to Paris to demonstrate exactly what the French musicians lacked. Predictably, some critics regarded this as a challenge to their national pride. They attacked the American orchestra for its cold, military precision and said they much preferred the freedom of their own orchestras.

In 1978 Solti and the Chicago Symphony were back in Europe a third time, giving concerts at the leading festivals in Edinburgh, Lucerne, Berlin and Salzburg. Solti is a highly competitive man and proud of his achievements. It must have given him special pleasure to appear with his own orchestra at Salzburg where his sole rival, Karajan, is king, and where the Vienna Philharmonic and the Berlin Philharmonic have been the resident orchestras year after year. Salzburg is one of the European musical summits, and Solti had reached it at last with his own orchestra.

The other important foreign tour was the 1977 trip to Japan. As might be expected, audiences and critics were stunned:

> No orchestra in Japan can produce the combination of resources of this one...Japanese critical reviews always tend to be harsh on American orchestras. But the Chicago Symphony, for the first time, produced a richness and dimension of sound that made my skin crawl, and that will never be reproduced, no matter how advanced audio products become." (Junichiro Kawazuka, *Nihon Keizai Shimbun*)

Although in the long run such tours are extremely important for the reputation of the orchestra, they are, as has already been mentioned, enormously expensive. Many people believe that the State Department, in order to foster good will and demonstrate American cultural sophistication, bears the cost of all these junkets. However, this is by no means always the case. With so many American orchestras demanding the chance to travel, government funds have been scarce, and ambitious orchestras have been forced to find other ways to finance such ventures. For the Chicago Symphony's 1978 European tour, the City of Chicago put up $150,000, believing the orchestra's presence abroad would be good for the city's image. After all, in some countries it is still believed that gangsters run wild in the streets of Chicago, an impression that, needless to say, is not good for business. For this same tour the orchestra also received a substantial contribution from the Continental Illinois National Bank. In return, the bank used one of the orchestra's London concerts as a kind of gala party for the opening of its new London branch. Obviously such helpful financing must be the result of hard work by the board of the orchestra. At the same time, fund raising would not stand a chance if the product were not superlative. By 1978 Solti and the Chicago Symphony were universally acknowledged as being not merely superlative, but in nearly every respect in which orchestras and conductors are evaluated, unbeatable.

Besides the glamorous foreign touring, the orchestra travels frequently within the United States. A subscription series of ten concerts is given every season in Milwaukee (just ninety miles away), in addition to the orchestra's more irregular appearances throughout its home state of Illinois. Occasionally the Chicago Symphony will travel further afield, to the west coast or to Canada, but the most important annual concerts away from Chicago are undoubtedly those which take place in New York City. These triumphant Carnegie Hall concerts, of which there have been two to three twice each season since Solti arrived in

Chicago, have done more for the image and reputation of the orchestra than any of its other activities. It certainly helps that Solti presents such blockbusters as *Das Rheingold*, Act III from *Götterdämmerung*, and Mahler and Bruckner symphonies; nonetheless, there is an enormous depth of appreciation for conductor and orchestra in New York that does not exist to quite the same degree anywhere else. A hostile critic might argue that this is because at the time of the first concerts there was no competition. The Boston Symphony and the New York Philharmonic were struggling with conductors, the Cleveland Orchestra faded into the background with the death of Szell, and the most durable conductor-orchestra association among the Big Five (Ormandy and the Philadelphia) was taken for granted. But this objection can hardly be sustained considering the fact that Solti and the Chicago Symphony have created a sensation every year since 1969. Audiences at these concerts often go wild to the point of hysteria. After a performance of the Mahler Fifth, Winthrop Sargeant made this observation in the *New Yorker*:

> The conclusion of the final *Allegro* was the occasion for the longest ovation I have ever seen any conductor receive (except possibly Herbert von Karajan) since the time of Toscanini. It would probably have gone all night but for the fact that Mr. Solti led his concertmaster off the stage.

The New York critics have a reputation for being rather tough, but for Solti and his orchestra from the Midwest they have generally gone along with the audiences. Harold Schonberg was especially effusive after a performance of Wagner's *Das Rheingold* in 1971:

> The climax of the New York orchestral season came tonight in Carnegie Hall, courtesy of Georg Solti and the Chicago Symphony Orchestra...The performance was completely sold out. Everybody went wild, and for good reason. It was an evening of greatness...a great opera played by a great orchestra under a great conductor. (New York *Times*)

Nor is there any sign that the New York critics have cooled over the years. After a performance of Brahms' *A German Requiem* in the spring of 1978, Raymond Ericson of the New York *Times* pronounced it "the best performance this writer has ever heard...Mr. Solti, with a superb orchestra and chorus at his command, seemed to do everything exactly right." (May 14, 1978)

New York is Mecca these days on the musical scene. It is the place where all the world's ranking orchestras feel compelled to appear regularly to prove to the folks back home that they are as good as they keep saying they are. For this reason, a New York concert can be a nerve-shattering experience. To fail in New York is to be put demonstrably in one's place in the scheme of things. But to succeed, as splendidly as Solti and his orchestra have done, is to know that one has really arrived.

While the extra effort that goes into New York concerts undeniably makes for special performances, a few listeners and even some members of the orchestra feel that the competitiveness and the ovations have gotten in the way of an honest assessment of what an orchestra can do. One Chicago Symphony player expressed this sentiment in a letter to the Chicago *Tribune* in 1974:

> When an orchestra can bring down the house at Carnegie Hall with a programme of Mozart or Haydn, we can then be convinced of our success. Instead, the Chicago Symphony Orchestra is sounding more and more like the brass brand at the half-time show of Maestro Solti's football game.

Solti, however, is not oblivious to the liabilities of performing in New York:

> The orchestra still suffers a lot from that "second city" complex. Carnegie Hall is still the magic name, and we are so obsessed with conquering Carnegie, I have to tell the players, "Don't look at the crowds, try to relax, it's just another concert." But it never works. In New York the orchestra plays with a tension that surprises even me. I constantly have to make them play softer than they do at home. (*New York,* September 20, 1976)

Unfortunately, the Chicago Symphony's regular fall and spring visits to New York have had to be reduced to a single series each season. Even for superheroes, frequent trips to New York have become almost prohibitively expensive. The orchestra's going rate for an appearance on the road, $25,000, is a fair indication of the cost of moving over 106 players and all their instruments from one city to another. And there are simply not enough places and organizations able to pay that kind of money; no matter how illustrious the orchestra, ticket sales do not cover costs. The Chicago Symphony itself finances its New York concerts, and although each performance is sold out months in advance, there is still a deficit.

Back home, Chicago audiences and press have enthusiastically endorsed the superstar status granted the Symphony in New York. The one glaring exception has been Claudia Cassidy, the notorious critic who single-handedly forced Rafael Kubelik from his post with the orchestra in 1953. Of an opera performance conducted by Solti she observed that the Maestro was smiling when the ensemble was so bad he should have been cutting his throat. Being the hyper-sensitive man he is, Solti has not forgotten this review: "I really have a hate for that woman. I wouldn't be in Chicago today if she were still writing." (*New Yorker* Profile, May 27, 1974) But with the departure of Claudia Cassidy from the daily press in Chicago, Solti has had little to fear. Robert C. Marsh of the Chicago *Sun-Times* is now the most influential of the city's critics and he has been lavish in his praise of Solti from the beginning. In Solti's first season he described a performance of Stravinsky's *Rite of Spring* as "the most perfect realization of this music I have ever encountered." (February 27, 1970)

It should be noted that Marsh is a Toscanini admirer of many decades standing, and that he approvingly sets Solti squarely in that tradition. The more rhapsodic Giulini he relates to Toscanini's old nemesis Wilhelm Furtwängler.

Not surprisingly, then, Marsh has been especially un-charitable in his reviews of Giulini's Chicago concerts.

Thomas Willis, music critic of the Chicago *Tribune* un-til 1977 and now a member of the Faculty of Music at Northwestern University, has also supported Solti through-out his Chicago tenure, although both Willis and Marsh have been critical of Solti's frequent and extended depar-tures from Chicago, or, as Willis has put it, his "absentee landlordism." (The Chicago *Guide*, May 1971) Another Chicago critic, Karen Monson, formerly of the *Daily News* and an early Solti enthusiast, holds the conductor in some-thing approaching awe. She was the only American jour-nalist to accompany Solti on his historic return to Hungary with the Vienna Philharmonic in the spring of 1978, and she sent back detailed reports on the conductor's every word.

Solti has been consistently criticized in Chicago for his long absences and for the conservatism of his repertoire, but as far as his conducting is concerned he has been among friends. Nearly all observers agree that this is the golden age of the Chicago Symphony and that Solti is responsible for it. Solti himself is not unaware of this fact. Recently, he responded to the suggestion that he ought to show more gratitude to Chicago by declaring: "The city should erect a statue to me. Eight years ago when I came, the orchestra was virtually unknown, nationally and internationally. We accomplished a small miracle."

In spite of Solti's unbecoming immodesty, he is right, as most members of the orchestra would readily agree. Many of them might prefer other conductors in this or that piece, or even in general, but they respect the standards Solti has imposed on them and the acclaim they now enjoy. They also appreciate the substantial increase in their paycheques. In 1973 the starting salary for a member of the Chicago Symphony was $320 a week. Five years later it was $500. And the majority of the players have negotiated salaries far beyond that. Moreover, recording fees account for another $3,000 - $5,000 annually per musician. Under Martinon, the orchestra's recording career was at its lowest ebb—its records did not sell and no company would risk making more. With the upsurge of the orchestra's reputation under Solti, record producers now come begging. At the moment the Chicago Symphony records regularly with Solti for Decca-London, with Levine for RCA, Barenboim and Abbado for DG, and Previn for Angel. Giulini was also recording with the orchestra for Angel and DG, but can no longer do so under the terms of his new contract with Los Angeles.

It is also due to Solti that the orchestra has returned to regular radio broadcasting after a long silence. At last count 300 stations were broadcasting its concerts, and for the players this means about $2,000 more each season. (Incidentally, the broadcasts are made possible not from earned income on the sale of the programmes, but by a grant from Standard Oil of Indiana which donates $500,000 yearly. Standard certainly could find other uses for its money were it not for the orchestra's current prestige.) Add to that the earnings ($1,000 per player) from a recently instituted series of television taping sessions for Unitel, and it is not surprising that the orchestra is all smiles on the subject of Solti. Not only are the members showered with praise at every turn from audiences and reviewers, they are remunerated most handsomely. The lowliest member of the ensemble makes in excess of $32,000 a season.

In the spring of 1978 there were rumblings from Chicago that Solti was "out to get" some of the older members of the orchestra. There is no mandatory retirement age, and forty players were then at least sixty years old. When he first arrived on the scene in 1969 Solti expressed concern about the average age of the orchestra, but nearly ten years later and with a much greater reputation to maintain, Solti was deeply worried. The Chicago Symphony runs its own training orchestra for young professionals—the Civic Orchestra of Chicago—and many of these players do graduate into the parent orchestra. At present nearly fifty percent of the musicians in the Chicago Symphony are alumni of the Civic Orchestra. Nevertheless, if permanent members of the Chicago Symphony are not ready to leave, it is difficult to move in young players. These older members are well protected from the prejudices of the music director, as Jean Martinon found to his chagrin. Yet festering animosities between certain aging players and the conductor are bound to cause trouble one day.

This problem is by no means unique to Chicago. It is inevitable in any symphony orchestra and must be ironed out with skilful diplomacy on all sides. Knowing John Edwards' track record, it will be surprising indeed if amicable solutions are not found in Chicago. It should be stressed that Solti's revitalization of the Chicago Symphony never involved wholesale changes of personnel. What he achieved, he achieved with the members of Martinon's orchestra. In fact, when Solti took over, eleven of the fifteen principals from the Reiner days were among the players. Solti's success in Chicago has not been gained by bringing in new musicians, although by now there are quite a few Solti appointments in the orchestra; rather, it has been the result of his ability to get the best out of what was already there.

In 1982 Solti will likely bring to an end his association with the Chicago Symphony. He has never liked the administrative aspects of the job: planning a season, auditioning players, overseeing youth concerts and chamber music, meeting with business and political leaders for fund-raising purposes, and all the other duties that go into being a music director but which take time away from conducting. Solti will be seventy years old in 1982 and more concerned than ever about making the most of the years left to him as a conductor. Perhaps a formula can be worked out whereby Solti is given the title of Conductor Laureate, as Bernstein was by the New York Philharmonic. He will then be able to conduct and record with the orchestra on a regular basis, while leaving the responsibilities of the music director to a successor. But a great deal will depend on who that successor is. He may not want Solti looking over his shoulder, muttering about how the orchestra has been allowed to deteriorate, basking in hysterical ovations every time he makes a guest appearance. For his part, Solti might find it impossible to keep his nose out of the affairs of the orchestra. There is a disquieting precedent for just such a situation. When Stokowski stepped down as Music Director of the Philadelphia Orchestra to be succeeded by Eugene Ormandy, he continued to appear as guest conductor. But he also persisted in behaving as if the orchestra were still his. It was an untenable situation for Ormandy, and Stokowski was invited to sever his connection. Such was the depth of the unpleasantness that Stokowski did not return at all until twenty years had passed.

Whatever the future holds for Chicago, Solti will not be forgotten. He has made more recordings with the orchestra than any previous music director. Among the recording firsts are: a complete Beethoven symphony cycle, a complete Beethoven piano concerto cycle, and a complete opera recording. The awards that have been showered on orchestra and conductor—a Grand Prix du Disque for the Mahler Fifth, three Grammys for the Mahler Eighth and one for the Mahler Seventh, three more for the Berlioz *Symphonie Fantastique*, and more still for the two Beethoven sets—will also serve as lasting reminders of Solti's achievements.

Because of Solti, the Chicago Symphony today, if not the best orchestra anywhere, has only one or two possible rivals. But if Solti has been good for the orchestra, they have helped him too. When he arrived in Chicago he was universally admired for his opera work. The recorded *Ring* cycle and his accomplishments at Covent Garden in the sixties were impressive credentials. Nevertheless, he had yet to really prove himself on the concert platform. In fact, it was a novelty for him to be able to work with a first-class orchestra for a six week stretch several times each season, knowing he could look forward to doing the same thing for years to come. He found himself having to learn all kinds of new repertoire, including many of the Mahler symphonies. His symphonic output on records was also very small in 1969. Now his catalogue is huge, and his versions are often mentioned as among the best available. It is not an exaggeration to say that Solti became a great concert conductor in Chicago; still, he needed the enormous ability of the Chicago Symphony to reach that goal.

What is it about the combination of Solti and the Chicago Symphony that has bowled over music-lovers everywhere? Granted, he makes them play well, but surely they have enough ability and pride to do that anyway. Exactly what does he get out of them that seems to suggest he has powers bordering on the magical?

Solti has said that to be a conductor one must have imagination and also the power to make an orchestra play what one imagines — a straightforward comment, but also a shrewd one. By way of example, Solti has often cited his teacher in Budapest, Ernst von Dohnányi. One of the greatest pianists of all time, he could give an overwhelming recital one day, and then conduct the worst orchestral concert the next. He had no talent for conveying his enormous insight to an orchestra. Say what you will about Solti, he knows what he wants and he knows how to get it. However, this is true of all successful conductors and one must go further to explain how Solti obtains what *he* wants.

Energy is crucial. It is exhausting keeping after an orchestra day in and day out, always insisting on perfection, always demanding the players' undivided attention. And Solti has this kind of energy in abundance. In addition, a conductor must be resourceful and diplomatic. It is not enough to repeat over and over, "That's not right. Do it again." The players only become tired, frustrated and ultimately antagonized. Rather, a good conductor must be absolutely precise about what is wrong—is the passage too loud, too soft, too fast, too slow, too penetrating, too expressive? He must isolate the problem by having the offending instruments play alone, and perhaps more slowly. If the strings are at fault, perhaps a change in bowing will help. Again Solti is good at this aspect of his job.

It is also of the utmost importance that the conductor have something to offer at the concert beyond time-beating competence. Some conductors put all their energy into rehearsal and then rely totally on the orchestra's memory during performance. But Solti's painstaking vigilance never abates. If anything, he conveys even more tension at the concert. It is partly the way he sets himself on the podium, tense and poised like a runner at the starting-line. It is also his eyes and facial muscles, both of which impart an infectious alertness. Regardless of how tired the players may be and whatever their domestic problems, Solti's presence is so compelling it is difficult for the musicians to do otherwise than to give him 100 percent. This unique ability to project the authority of his personality accounts in large measure for Solti's tremendous success in communicating his vision of the music to an orchestra. He convinces the musicians by means of his persuasive presence and also by means of the previous experiences they have had with him that he is thoroughly prepared, that he is deeply committed to the music, and that he will lead them safely through the score.

Solti's methods, however, are not so successful with orchestras other than his own. The frequently-voiced criticism from players about Solti when he guest conducts is that "he comes on too strong," or that he "bullies" them, not rudely but persistently. Often their first reaction is to shut him out and lie back, doing what they are told but without any enthusiasm. Solti then seems to the audience to be over-conducting, and labouring mightily to bring forth very little.

The rapport between the Chicago Symphony and Solti owes something as well to the influences of Reiner and

Martinon on the orchestra. It is obvious from the pre-Solti recordings that the brass section was at once enormously strong, clear and well-balanced. The playing of the brass in the Reiner Wagner and Strauss recordings is remarkable for its agility and security of attack and intonation. But the sound also has a darkness more commonly found in Europe. The same comments could be made about the winds and strings. Solti has always preferred an opulent sound. At the same time, he is fanatical in his concern for rhythmic clarity. This is why the Vienna Philharmonic, for all its fabled power and richness, has been a problem for Solti. To his ears, the musicians are sloppy about rhythmic matters, moving far too sluggishly from note to note. In Chicago, Solti found the strong, lush sound of the Vienna Philharmonic, although not the distinctive instrumental timbres of that orchestra, coupled with the most sophisticated rhythmic sense he could ask for. It is no wonder he has revelled in the playing of the Chicago Symphony.

Comparisons are now possible between the Vienna Philharmonic and the Chicago Symphony playing the same repertoire on records under Solti. The Beethoven symphonies he has recorded with both orchestras, Nos. 3, 5 and 7, are not the best examples because the Chicago versions are uncharacteristically dull in performance and recording. The Wagner overtures are more illuminating. Solti's old versions with the Vienna Philharmonic are excitingly played and recorded, but the new ones are even better in terms of intonation and precision, while no less gripping. For some conductors, the Vienna Philharmonic would be enough. For Solti, with his never-to-be-forgotten exposure to Toscanini's criteria, the Chicago Symphony is able to provide more of what he hears when he studies a score. In this orchestra, Solti has found the ideal instrument for the realization of his musical ideas. And the players responded as readily as they did because he did not need to ask them to change their style of playing. The "Reiner Sound" is essentially the same as the "Solti Sound."

Whatever the reasons for the tremendous success of the Chicago Symphony/Solti marriage, it is a unique and fortuitous alliance. As the tenth anniversary approaches, perhaps the city fathers should give serious consideration after all to erecting a statue of Solti. He might decide to stay a little longer.

4
Forging Decca's Ring

In 1958, when the *Ring* project was set in motion by Decca Records, Solti was still largely unknown outside Germany. By the time this mammoth enterprise was completed, in 1965, he was a figure of international stature. These recordings established him as being, beyond any doubt, an important conductor.

It is hard to believe now that there was a time when no complete recording of the *Ring* existed. The four operas, or music dramas as Wagner preferred to call them, comprise one of the undisputed masterpieces in the history of music. Yet half a century passed before they attracted the active attention of any record company. There are five or six complete *Ring* recordings on the market today, but in 1958 there was not even one. The work is huge both in terms of the forces involved—sixteen harps plus batteries of anvils are added to an already immense orchestra in *Das Rheingold,* and in terms of sheer length—a recording of the *Ring* requires four large boxed sets containing from three to six LP's each. No company had ever attempted anything on this scale before, and was especially reluctant to do so when there was no hard evidence that a market existed anyway. In addition, casting was a problem. Critics had been complaining for years about the dearth of real Wagnerian voices. Where were the heldentenors, heldenbaritones and leather-lunged Brünnhilde's to be found?

Nonetheless, at the urging of producer John Culshaw, Decca decided to take the plunge in 1957. Or at least it decided to take the first step. *Die Walküre* was the most popular of the *Ring* music dramas and had been recorded once already by another company. Decca now planned to produce its own *Walküre* and, if sales were encouraging, to go on to do the other three parts of the *Ring*. In order to guarantee the success of the recording, Decca intended to use the universally-acclaimed Queen of Wagnerian sopranos, Norwegian-born Kirsten Flagstad. Unfortunately, Flagstad was unwilling to take on the entire role of Brünnhilde at that late stage in her career and, in any case, wanted to sing the part of Sieglinde too. After many months of negotiation, the company was forced either to accept Flagstad on her own terms or to do without her. Having committed itself to some sort of start on the *Ring*, and believing that the project was doomed without Flagstad, Decca went ahead with an impossible mixture: Act I of *Die Walküre* with Flagstad as Sieglinde and Hans Knappertsbusch conducting; scenes from Act II with Flagstad as Brünnhilde and again with Knappertsbusch; and the whole of Act III with Flagstad as Brünnhilde and Solti conducting. The only participants common to all three parts were producer John Culshaw and the members of the Vienna Philharmonic Orchestra. With this kind of hodgepodge and with an incomplete *Walküre* emerging as a result, the notion of recording the entire *Ring* seemed far-fetched indeed.

But Culshaw and his superiors at Decca were undaunted. The *Walküre* experience had taught them a great deal about how to handle such projects. More importantly, market response was sufficient to indicate a widespread interest in large chunks of Wagner on records. Culshaw therefore suggested going on to *Das Rheingold* which, unlike *Walküre,* had never been recorded before. Also in *Rheingold's* favour was the fact that it had neither a soprano nor a heldentenor problem and that it was the shortest of the *Ring* music dramas. Decca's management still believed the magic of the Flagstad name was an essential ingredient in the production, and as there was no major role for her in *Rheingold,* Culshaw managed to persuade her to undertake the part of Fricka. In his published account of Decca's *Ring* recording, *Ring Resounding,* Culshaw explains why he devoted so much of his time to dealing with the sensitive and unpredictable Flagstad:

> In retrospect it may seem that we paid an inordinate amount of attention to persuading Flagstad to sing what is, after all, a small role. There were two main reasons, and the first was commercial. In 1958 the name Flagstad was still a very powerful draw for the Wagner audience, and nobody at that stage could possibly predict whether *Rheingold* was going to be an expensive success or an expensive flop. Anything which might contribute to its sales potential was of importance to those who were investing money in such an unknown starter. Had she refused, we would have gone ahead without her because by then it was too late to withdraw. The other reason was that those of us who dreamed that *Rheingold* might be the beginning of the first recorded *Ring* wanted above all that Flagstad should be a part of it, no matter how modest, for we sensed that time was running out for her.

In fact, Flagstad died in 1962 just after the completion of Decca's *Siegfried,* the first of it's *Ring* recordings in which she was not involved. By that time, though, after the extraordinary success of *Rheingold,* the participation of a Flagstad was no longer crucial.

How did Solti become involved in such an historic project? Surely Decca, in its concern with commercial viability, would have wanted a conductor possessing both an international reputation and a recognized affinity for Wagner. In 1958 Solti was all but unknown to the record-buying public. However, John Culshaw had seen Solti conduct *Die Walküre* in Munich in 1950:

> It affected me more than any other Wagner performance I had ever heard. It was not the best I had heard, but it was the most unified; it was a conception; and it was theatre. (*Ring Resounding*)

And Culshaw was not the only one at Decca impressed by Solti. In the mid-forties, Maurice Rosengarten, the head of the company, had spotted Solti and signed him to a contract. By the mid-fifties, Decca had recorded Solti in a fairly sizable number of symphonic pieces, even though the conductor was best-known for his work in the opera house. It seemed only a matter of time before Solti would record some opera for Decca. Moreover, it appeared likely that the opera would be by Wagner, in view of Solti's growing reputation with the composer's works. The Vienna Philharmonic was under contract to the record company as well, and there was never any doubt that the *Ring* would be made with this world-renowned orchestra which was, and still is, the pit orchestra for the Vienna State Opera. The combination of Solti and the Vienna Philharmonic appeared inevitable.

But the conductor Decca had in mind for the *Ring* project was Hans Knappertsbusch. His *Parsifal* performances at Bayreuth had become legend, and he was equally respected for his interpretations of the other Wagner music dramas. However, like many conductors, Knapperstbusch, who could be a spellbinder in the opera house or the concert hall, was a *Kapellmeister* in the studio. Also, if Culshaw is to be believed, Knappertsbusch really did not want to record. He hated rehearsing and he hated retakes:

> The truth is that Knappertsbusch took very badly to recording conditions, and no matter what we did, the genius which he so certainly revealed in the theatre refused to come alive in the studio...We tried to drag him, kicking and screaming, into the twentieth century of the gramophone record, the era of the listener at home who hears without any visual aid and without the community of the theatre. It was an alien world for him. (*Ring Resounding*)

By contrast, Solti's work with Culshaw on Act III of *Walküre* had been immensely satisfying. Solti is exactly the sort of man who can exploit the potential of the recording process. A tireless ball of energy and a perfectionist, he works quickly and responds well to requests for retakes. No matter how many times he goes over a passage, it never became routine or dull. Culshaw wanted his *Ring* cycle to have all the electricity of a first-class, live performance; he wanted it to be a theatrical experience. With Solti as conductor he was assured of the realization of these ideals.

While the artistic and commercial success of Decca's *Ring* project confirms the wisdom of the choice of Solti as conductor, it was still a calculated risk in 1958. Solti was largely inexperienced in conducting *Das Rheingold*. And when he came to record *Siegfried* and *Götterdämmerung*, he had yet to conduct live performances of either composition.

It makes far greater sense to record a work immediately after a series of public performances. This procedure saves on costly rehearsal time and ensures that the conductor has a firm conception of a piece as a complete entity when he comes into the studio. When one considers that Herbert von Karajan, with the Vienna State Opera, was then performing the *Ring* cycle works Decca planned on recording initially and that, in fact, the same orchestra, the Vienna Philharmonic, and many of the same singers Decca contracted were involved in Karajan's performances, it seems strange that the eminent Austrian conductor was not chosen for the record company's *Ring* project. Whereas Solti was just beginning to make his way, Karajan was well-established as a superstar. He had conducted the *Ring* at Bayreuth with enormous success and he was currently conducting and producing it at the State Opera in Vienna, where he had been Artistic Director since 1956. He was the logical choice both artistically and commercially for any *Ring* cycle to be made in Vienna beginning in 1958. Furthermore, Culshaw was later to embark on a series of opera recordings, including *Aïda, Otello, Die Fledermaus* and *Carmen*, for Decca with Karajan and the Vienna Philharmonic. In a letter to this author, Culshaw offered the following explanation:

> The decision to record the *Ring* was taken after the huge success of the Solti Flagstad *Walküre* Act III which was made in 1957. At that time Karajan was under exclusive contract to EMI, and did not come to Decca until either 1958 or 1959. (His first Decca recording was *Zarathustra*). But Solti was a front-runner in any case because — quite apart from artistic considerations — he was developing a truly international name. (November 20, 1978)

Karajan did record the *Ring* later, for Deutsche Grammophon, in connection with performances given at the Salzburg Easter Festival.

Even on the eve of recording *Das Rheingold,* there were those who thought the whole idea was ridiculous. One such sceptic was Walter Legge, Culshaw's opposite number at EMI. Culshaw and Solti have both told the story of Legge's grave doubts with enormous pleasure, although Culshaw identifies Legge only as "a very distinguished colleague." Here is Solti's account:

> I remember meeting him at the bar of the Imperial Hotel in Vienna on the eve of the recording of *Das Rheingold.* "Well, what are you doing here?" he asked. "We start recording *Das Rheingold* tomorrow morning." "*Das Rheingold*..." He was astonished, "it is a very beautiful opera, but you won't sell a single record!" Since 1958 we sold more than 300,000 sets! For him this was impossible to imagine. This great discoverer of talent had Furtwängler and Flagstad under contract and it never occured to him to record the Tetralogy with them. He was convinced that such a recording would not sell: *Die Walküre* or *Tristan* maybe (he in fact recorded these) but *Das Rheingold, Siegfried* and *Götterdämmerung* were to him synonymous to financial disaster. (*Le Point* No. 133, April 7, 1975)

Decca's *Das Rheingold* was a sensation when it was finally released. Its commercial and artistic success proved that a market existed for Wagner operas on record. Listeners were astounded by the incredible sound. This was in the early days of stereo recording, when companies were rushing into the market with the most spectacular effects they could devise. The dynamic range, the immediacy of sound, the timbral accuracy of each instrument and the overall realism in the *Rheingold* recording appealed not only to Wagner buffs and opera fans, but to a new breed altogether, which was just beginning to have an impact on the record industry. These were the audiophiles or hi-fi nuts. *Rheingold* became the favourite demonstration record to show off expensive amplifiers and speakers.

Die Walküre is the second of the four *Ring* music dramas, and one might have expected Decca to tackle it next. But since the company already had generous excerpts from *Walküre* on the market, it decided to leave *Walküre* until later and to proceed with *Siegfried* instead. Yet four years were to elapse before the work was finally recorded. Other opera projects in more advanced stages of production had to be given priority, and Decca also had to deal with an almost insuperable problem casting the title role. Although Wolfgang Windgassen was ultimately to make the recording, Culshaw was against him initially and explored every other possibility. At one stage, Culshaw decided to take a chance on a promising but inexperienced young tenor. The voice was right for the part, and while the man had never sung the role, he agreed to learn it with Decca's coaches under Solti's supervision.

The recording sessions were scheduled for May of 1962, but as late as mid-April Decca's budding heldentenor did not yet know the part. Still, the company persisted with its novice until three sessions with the orchestra forced everyone concerned to admit defeat. Siegfried would have to be replaced. All the material recorded thus far was useless, of course, and with no Siegfried in sight the entire project seemed doomed. The only way out was to get hold of the only tenor currently singing the title role on a regular basis in 1962: Wolfgang Windgassen. Windgassen knew that Culshaw had passed him over, and he was further aware of Culshaw's casting fiasco. Was the tenor likely to want to help Culshaw salvage the Siegfried project? As it happened, Windgassen was more than willing to step in, but his agent insisted on making the most of Decca's plight. The fee demanded was so high Culshaw was again convinced that there would never be a *Siegfried* recording. Frantic contract negotiations continued right into the recording session in which Windgassen was scheduled to appear. Finally, the lure of being the first-recorded Siegfried won Windgassen over, and he overruled his agent.

Siegfried turned out to be as fine an achievement as

Rheingold had been. Windgassen may not be the Siegfried of one's dreams—opera is still waiting for that—but he is competent, and the Act III duet with Birgit Nilsson is electrifying. Overall, the casting is superb with Hans Hotter as Wotan, Gustav Neidlinger as Alberich and Gerhard Stolze as Mime. For many years Stolze was one of the greatest singing actors on the operatic scene. Although his voice was not beautiful in a conventional sense, his powers of characterization were amazing. More amazing still is the fact that he recorded the part of the dwarf while still receiving treatment for a devastating attack of polio.

Two years after *Siegfried,* Culshaw and his crew returned to the Sofiensaal in Vienna to record *Götterdämmerung.* Before the sessions, Decca decided to provide optimum studio conditions and installed a great deal of new recording gear, within a newly-constructed control room. How strange that in old Vienna, a city where some of the best concert halls in the world may be found, the ideal recording location should turn out to be a dance hall! The fact is that engineers can capture the sound of the Vienna Philharmonic far better in the Sofiensaal than in any concert hall. The numerous outstanding recordings made in the Sofiensaal certainly bear this out.

The casting for Siegfried was carried over into *Götterdämmerung,* with Windgassen as Siegfried, Nilsson as Brünnhilde, Neidlinger as Alberich and, of course, Solti conducting. Outstanding additions to the ensemble were Dietrich Fischer-Dieskau as an unusually sympathetic Gunther, and Gottlob Frick, as black and menacing a bass voice as one could ever hope to hear, as the evil Hagen. By this time, Nilsson had become the indispensable component Flagstad had been when the *Ring* project was first discussed. In the roles of Brünnhilde and Isolde, Nilsson, with her power, beauty of tone and endurance, was matchless. No one could soar over a Wagner orchestra in full cry as she could. One of the great liabilities of the Karajan *Ring* cycle for DG recorded just a few years later is that it attempts to do without Nilsson. The substitutes, Régine Crespin in *Walküre* and Helga Dernesch in *Siegfried* and *Götterdämmerung,* for all their subtleties of interpretation, sound woefully overtaxed in comparison to Nilsson.

Solti's conducting is on an even higher level of achievement than it was for *Siegfried.* As Edward Greenfield observed, one finds, in *Götterdämmerung,* a Solti:

> ...revealing a warmth, a consideration for the singers' needs as well as the orchestra's which was not there before...now Solti builds his climaxes far more subtly, with — it now seems — more love than before, without losing the excitement that has always marked his Wagner conducting. (*High Fidelity/Musical America,* December 1965)

Following the completion of the first recorded *Götterdämmerung,* Decca had only to retrace its steps and do an entire *Walküre.* With the end of the cycle in sight, the record company lost no time, returning to the studios in Vienna only a little more than a year after *The Twilight of the Gods.* Birgit Nilsson was again Brünnhilde and once more at the top of her form. But Hans Hotter, as Wotan, was in the last stages of his career and the supercharged, large-scale concept of the performance severely taxed him. The choice of James King as Siegmund was also an unhappy one. King does not sing badly; it is just that he sings with no particular distinction. The ranking Siegmund in 1965 was Jon Vickers and he was soon to record the role with Karajan. Vicker's combination of musical insight and dramatic power is in a class all its own.

The completion of the first recorded *Ring* cycle was just cause for celebration. All those who participated in the project felt they had reached the end of an important journey. And indeed they had. The recordings received all the appropriate accolades in terms of reviews, prizes and sales figures, and they still stand today as one of the greatest achievements of the gramophone. While much of the credit must go to Solti and the Vienna Philharmonic, and to vocal stars of the magnitude of Birgit Nilsson, George London and Hans Hotter, it is John Culshaw who was ultimately responsible for the amazing sound of the recordings. He encouraged his forces to give their best and to master the many difficult passages in these works. The notoriously treacherous *Rheingold* Prelude, for example, can sound bad enough in the opera house, even though it is quiet music and disasters in performance are often partially covered by the noise of chattering and late arrivals. Culshaw's problem was to get all eight horns to play their successive solo entries perfectly in the same long take. The overlapping entries do not allow for editing.

While Culshaw's influence in the *Ring* recordings was extensive, it was not unusually so. It is in the nature of the recording medium in the second half of the twentieth century that the producer should have considerable input. He may have months of difficult work to do both before and after the sessions, and he often makes artistic decisions which normally one might expect to be the conductor's prerogative. It was Culshaw who sought out and auditioned the right kind of steerhorn for *Götterdämmerung,* and it was Culshaw too who called Bayreuth to try to resolve a textual ambiguity in the score of *Walküre.*

Because the Decca *Ring* recordings began at a time when Solti was just beginning to conduct performances of the cycle in the opera house, it might be argued that Culshaw was taking advantage of Solti's inexperience. No doubt there were matters Solti could have had more say in or dispatched more quickly had he been a more seasoned conductor of Wagner's music. On the other hand, the Decca *Ring* was not a live performance. It was a recording. And in matters concerning recorded sound Culshaw, not Solti, was the expert. The same distinction would have applied even if Toscanini or Karajan had been the conductor.

Since the *Ring* project stretched over a period of seven years, stylistic developments are evident in the work of certain performers. This is especially true of Solti, as many critics have been quick to note, for he was the only one involved at every stage of the cycle. And since *Walküre* was the last of the recordings, the most dramatic comparisons concern it and the 1957 excerpted version. Reviewing the complete *Walküre* in *High Fidelity*, Conrad L. Osborne was critical of Culshaw's elaborate special effects, but commented at length on Solti's improvement as a Wagner conductor. He found Solti less nervous and more controlled. Osborne also suggested that the new, improved Solti had become a better Wagner than a Verdi conductor:

> It is not my favourite kind of Wagner conduting, but to me it sounds involved, dramatically aware, in a way that his Verdi, for example, does not. (November 1966)

Other critics have been less favourably impressed by Solti's Wagner. Samuel Lipman, in an article entitled "Performing The Ring," from the January 1978 issue of *Commentary* extensively compared all the complete re-corded *Ring* cycles, from Solti through Karajan, Böhm, Furtwängler and Goodall. Here is what he had to say about Solti's conducting:

> He seems to have concentrated upon the exaggeration of short-range effects, and in particular, upon giving more prominence to the brass than has any other conductor. Many of these effects are startling, as are his frequent changes of tempo in excess of Wagner's indications. Regardless of the individual excellences of many passages, his *Ring* lacks an overall conception, whether musical or perhaps philosophical, that would go beyond the separate characters and their scenes to the question of the wider image of the entire work.

In *Music and Musicians* (March 1971), John Greenhalgh made similar observations, not about the Decca *Ring* but about Solti's Covent Garden performances of the cycle:

> It is to the conducting of Solti that some of the most adverse criticism of the *Ring* of the sixties must attach itself. Serious reservations must be made of Solti's overall interpretation. If one takes the *Ring* as a whole and excludes exceptional individual performances, it has been

basically disappointing. The *Ring* has not been heard as a single phrase of music lasting fourteen to fifteen hours in playing time. Yet it is as vital for a conductor to comprehend the *Ring* so, to hear it as a unity, and not to conduct it as four different operas, as it is for Brünnhilde to sing *Heil dir Sonne* in one breath. Covent Garden's recent *Rings* have contained orchestral sound of unsurpassed brilliance and climaxes of tremendous excitement. These and other merits of Solti's conducting are acknowledged and valued, but they are not what is required, first and foremost, when conducting the *Ring* in the opera house. They are no compensation for failing to sustain the whole work, despite its length. Under Solti the music of the *Ring* has been more a series of fragmented episodes, as he has moved from one climax to another, the threatening longueur in Wagner's music thereby kept at bay.

Later in the article it is suggested that Solti's problems with the *Ring* in the opera house can be traced to his earlier experience recording the work; that is, the stop-start studio approach prevents Solti from realizing the work as a total entity in the opera house.

It could be, however, that Lipman and Greenhalgh, while putting their fingers on one feature of Solti's conducting, have failed to interpret it correctly. From Solti's obvious obsession with detail they generalize that he has no view of the whole cycle. They further buttress this argument by pointing out that because the recording sessions stretched over a period of many years, the set could not project a unified view of the work. But what view of the whole can one expect to find? Wagner too laboured on the parts of the *Ring* for many years and there are many stylistic disparities in the music that attest to his development as a composer. Furthermore, there are differences in the orchestral sound appropriate to each of the *Ring* music dramas.

The drama is complex, sometimes confused and difficult to interpret, and Solti's problem is not that he hasn't grasped the unity of this manifold work; rather it is that his conception often entails interruption of the long line in the music, and this is a quite different criticism. Solti appears to have a very clear, firm idea of how he feels the music should be realized. He is totally in command of his orchestra and singers, from the first bar of *Rheingold* to the last bar of *Götterdämmerung*. He insists on accuracy of rhythm and intonation, yet his reading is by no means merely literal. On the contrary, it is highly dramatic. Lipman's and Greenhalgh's criticisms imply that Solti not only breaks the work up into sections for recording purposes, but that his interpretation is fragmented as well. This would suggest that there is a frequent loss of tension. Where does this occur? One can certainly point to many instances where it might be felt that the volume is too loud, the tempo too fast or the phrasing rather bland; still, these objections do not mean that the conductor lacks an overall conception. They mean only that one is in disagreement with that conception. Solti himself attempted to provide a clearer understanding of his ideas concerning the *Ring* in an April 7, 1975 interview for *Le Point*:

> My concept of the Tetralogy was not a "Germanic" concept, in the sense it was taken at that time. The *Ring* was conceived then as an enormous gloomy sonority—sombre, without rhythm, oceanic. According to what one called "tradition" it had to be misty, hazy. My concept was the opposite. I love clarity, rhythm, precision. It is in that spirit that I recorded the *Ring,* and I don't have the feeling at all that I maltreated the arrangement. Wagner's works are full of rhythm! It goes without saying that other interpretations are just as acceptable! Take, for example, four recordings of *Walküre:* one of Karajan, one of Furtwängler, one of Böhm, and mine. It is almost unbelievable that such a work could sound so completely different each time, while remaining so beautiful and moving!

This is a fair, although somewhat misleading assessment. Solti does explicitly reject the "Germanic tradition;" however, he is by no means radical—he is simply more precise in execution than most. The presence of the Vienna Philharmonic guarantees an authentic Wagner sound, with a tremendous weight when necessary and lovely tonal colouration, particularly in the strings. The orchestra is also capable of expressing the poetry of the music, but not often enough with Solti. In eliminating the gloom, he frequently does away with the poetry as well. This becomes especially obvious when one compares his recordings to those of Karajan and Furtwängler. In addition, both conductors maintain the flow of the music more consistently than does Solti. Unlike Solti, they "play across the bar lines." The forfeiting of Wagner's mystical side is the price Solti has willingly paid to do the *Ring* his way, and it is a valid way that pays dividends in matters of precision.

Would the more experienced Solti conduct the *Ring* differently were he to record the cycle today? Of course he would, and does in the opera house, but so too would any conductor twenty years later. He has admitted that he once found the cycle abhorrent because of its Nazi associations, but later changed his mind, even about that blond, blue-eyed Nazi prototype, Siegfried:

> I sympathize with Siegfried. He is abused by the dwarf but he loves animals. Through the bird he learns about the miracle of a woman. He didn't want the gold. He didn't want to fight. He is a superman but not a Nazi superman. You can of course read everything that way, but I think even in Shakespeare you can find supermen. And Wotan, he is killing the thing he loves. He is stupid. You cannot defend that either. (BBC interview, 1965)

In spite of any changes or improvements Solti might now consider appropriate, his *Ring* cycle for Decca remains a milestone in the history of recorded sound, and it is also one of his great achievements as a conductor. It faithfully reflects his musical attitude at a certain time in his career, and it is an attitude which commands respect.

5
The Beethoven Nine in Chicago

Beethoven's nine symphonies, taken as a unit, stand as one of the monuments of symphonic thought. If Haydn invented the symphony as a work for orchestra in four movements, Beethoven gave the form an unparalleled capacity to express the deepest and the most subtle of feelings. Moreover, Beethoven used symphonic form with infinite resourcefulness. Each of the nine symphonies is a unique entity, different from the others both musically and emotionally. In each, Beethoven set himself new problems and then solved them in new ways.

Consequently, the Beethoven symphonies are an essential part of any conductor's repertoire. He generally learns the works during his student days and wrestles with them throughout his career. But he is one of the élite indeed if he emerges from the struggle with glory. During the past half century, although many conductors have played these pieces time and again, only the performances of Toscanini, Weingartner, Furtwängler, Mengelberg, Klemperer, Szell and Karajan are memorable. While one or two others might be added to the list depending on personal bias, these men are the most widely heralded interpreters of the complete cycle. They are also, of course, among the most celebrated conductors generally. In other words, almost all of the conductors we call "great" have made their mark with the Beethoven Nine. The exceptions, Stokowski, Beecham and Koussevitzky among them, are few.

Solti himself readily points out that he came to the conducting of the Beethoven symphonies rather late in his career, and really did not have much concentrated experience with them until he took over the Chicago Symphony. The first Beethoven symphony he conducted was the Seventh, in Munich in 1946. In the course of his tenure there at the Bavarian State Opera he performed all the symphonies except the Ninth. His chance to do that work came finally in Frankfurt during the 1950's when he was Music Director of the Opera. Solti's concert work at Covent Garden was intermittent and never focussed on Beethoven; however in Chicago he was invited not only to play but to record all nine symphonies. Solti had made a recording of the Fourth with the London Philharmonic in 1950, and of the Third, Fifth and Seventh with the Vienna Philharmonic in 1958/59, but a complete cycle for posterity was a special occasion. In a conversation with music critic William Mann published on disc as part of the boxed set in the U.K., Solti remarks that every conductor should record the nine symphonies three times in his career: first, when he is young, about thirty—"*Sturm und Drang*" performances very likely, according to Solti; second, when he is in the middle of his career, around fifty years old; and finally, if he has time, when he is about seventy. Solti recorded nearly half the symphonies fairly early in his career, but he was into his sixties before the chance came to do a complete cycle. With his prestige and energy, he will almost certainly do at least one more.

Solti's early Beethoven recordings, tremendously vigorous, loud, fast and exciting performances with some wonderful playing on the Vienna Philharmonic recordings, are aptly characterized as *Sturm und Drang*. By contrast, the later recordings with the Chicago Symphony are energetic, but usually slower, quieter and generally the work of a more mature conductor. Still, there are enough miscalculations and inconsistencies to suggest that Solti's work with the Nine is still in progress.

In his conversation with William Mann, Solti singles out Toscanini as the most important influence on his approach to conducting Beethoven. Above all, he says, it was

Toscanini's "desperate seriousness" which impressed him. Toscanini was always working, always pouring over the score, while Solti was at that time "lazy and easy-going." In his younger days, Solti supported Toscanini's view that the Beethoven symphonies should be played fast, in accordance with the metronome markings, with great power and with a single tempo maintained throughout whole movements. Only much later did Solti seriously consider Furtwängler's much more flexible and personal approach to Beethoven.

Solti now feels the "truth for Beethoven" lies somewhere between the conceptions of these two conductors, and he has tried to find that middle way. In fact, the predominately moderate tempos of the Chicago Symphony Beethoven cycle are departures from the Toscanini ideal, although they still retain something of the Italian conductor's obsession with precision and intensity. But it could hardly be said that these performances represent a move towards the Furt-wängler approach. Furtwängler's Beethoven was charac-terized, above all, by freedom of tempo; it was notable for its spiritual and poetic qualities rather than for its precision. Also, his best performances exhibited a delightful in-evitability and spontaneity. The music seemed to be ad-vancing according to an irresistible logic while at the same time sounding fresh and alive. Such descriptions do not readily come to mind when listening to Solti's Beethoven. Even in conversation about the symphonies, Solti seems primarily concerned with technical problems.

Nevertheless, Solti's cycle has its own fine qualities. Above all, a wonderful authority is evident throughout; here is a master conductor who knows exactly what he wants and who has sufficient force of personality to persuade the musicians to give it to him. Furthermore, Solti frequently achieves first-rate ensemble playing, particularly in matters of rhythm. Rhythmic figures which often cause problems in performances even by good conductors and orchestras are never carelessly rendered by Solti's players. Solti's honest interpretation—his strict obedience to the letter of the score—is equally admirable. Every repeat in every movement is observed; all *sforzandi* are played with the same intensity; even traditional alterations to the score are cast aside in favour of the original.

However these performances do have their shortcomings. They were recorded over a period of about two years in three different locations: first the Ninth Symphony at the Krannert Centre in Chicago; next the Sixth and Seventh Symphonies in the Sofiensaal, Vienna; and then the rest in the Medina Temple, Chicago. The Medina Temple recordings are the worst: there is little resonance with the result that the strings sound as if they are forcing their tone almost constantly, and the woodwinds lose their individual colours. This ambience is particularly unfortunate because it reinforces what is least admirable in Solti's conducting.

In determining where to lay the blame for the poor sound, one must take into consideration: 1) the sound of the hall as it affects the performance being recorded, 2) the sound of the hall as it affects the performance we hear, 3) the sound produced by the engineers (including the sound of the hall, microphone placement, mixing, pressing, etc.) as it affects the performance we hear, and 4) the sound intended by the conductor. If the Medina Temple recordings are compared to the recordings with the same orchestra at the Sofiensaal in Vienna, the superiority of the latter is undeniable: the orchestra has a much warmer sound, the strings are forcing far less and the winds have colour and individuality. The Krannert Centre recordings are also much better than the Medina in these respects. One might be led to conclude, then, that the inferior sound of the Medina recordings is either the fault of the hall or the engineers. Yet, throughout all these performances there remains, to a greater or lesser degree, a characteristic aggressiveness in Solti's conducting, sometimes appropriate and sometimes not. For this reason, one cannot indiscriminately attribute the particular quality of these recordings, or any recordings for that matter, to either the hall, the engineers, the conductor or the members of the orchestra who might not be able to cope with acoustics of the hall. It is a complex matter which must be constantly borne in mind. As far as the Medina performances are concerned, the sound would be a great impediment to anyone's Beethoven, and must certainly colour an appreciation of Solti's.

In any case, and for whatever reasons, while he aims at a middle road between Toscanini and Furtwängler, Solti consistently fails to offer the kind of insight and excitement achieved by either conductor. He is vigorous and intense, but the result is often far from exciting. There is a heaviness of rhythmic accentuation that destroys both continuity and forward motion. One has the feeling that Solti is trying too hard to keep his impetuosity in check, as if to prove how mature he has become. He seems to be saying to himself "no more headlong tempos, no more bombastic outbursts." And yet *Sturm und Drang* is part of his nature. To restrain himself as stringently as he does in his Beethoven cycle is to destroy the lifeblood of the music. Perhaps in his next recording of the symphonies Solti should worry less about Toscanini and Furtwängler, and aim at a more satisfying balance between his own heart and mind.

Symphony No. 1 in C major Op. 21

Beethoven's First Symphony is often treated as an early work: more "Mozartean" or "Haydnesque" than "Beethovenian." It is generally felt that the real Beethoven does not emerge until the *Eroica* wherein one can recognize the fire, the pathos and the epic proportions lacking in the earlier symphonies. It is necessary, therefore, for a conductor preparing a performance of the First Symphony to consider it in relation to the remaining eight. The Beethoven of the C major was not yet the man who composed the others, either emotionally or musically, and the danger is that the conductor will blow up the slender proportions of this symphony to somehow speak the language of the *Eroica*, the Fifth or the Ninth. In fact, the C major is clearly modelled after the symphonies of the classical masters; it uses the standard Mozart-Haydn orchestra and the forms of its movements are almost textbook examples.

In his conversation with William Mann, Solti points to two features of the First to refute the claim that the composition is "Haydnesque:" the seventh chords which open the work, and the fragmentary statement of the main theme of the last movement. These are indeed unprecedented features for a classical symphony, but so too were numerous others like them in many of Haydn's symphonies; for instance, beginning with a timpani roll in No. 103 and using extra percussion in No. 100. Such innovations have nothing whatever to do with the essential style of the piece. In practical terms this means that Beethoven's First Symphony will not respond well to the extremes of tempo and dynamics which can be convincingly applied to his Third or Fifth Symphonies.

If, for example, a conductor uses a large string section appropriate to Wagner and Strauss, he obliterates the handful of woodwinds called for in the C major. Doubling the winds by way of compensation, as is often done today, only compounds the original mistake by creating much too big a sound. And if the *sforzando* accents are played in a violent manner appropriate to the Seventh, the modest proportions of the work are destroyed utterly. Beethoven's First Symphony is neither profound in expression nor revolutionary in technique, but it is often misunderstood by conductors overawed by the spirit of the later Beethoven.

Solti's performance is a compelling one. He is wonderfully attentive to every rhythmic detail, and scrupulously careful about every marking in the score. One hears no unmarked *ritardandi* or *accelerandi* here. Nothing is added to personalize the music or to make it superficially exciting. Nevertheless, his realization is not necessarily successful. Rejecting the notion that the C major is "Haydnesque,"

Solti uses what sounds like a very large string section. Coupled with a tendency to stress downbeats, the result is a relentless heaviness, even in the quick passages. The first themes in the *Allegro* sections of the first and last movements are absolutely classical in character, and when played with the appropriate lightness can be delightfully bouncy and infectious. Under the weight of sound Solti applies to this music, however, the fragile textures are beaten to a pulp. Although accents are laudably observed throughout the performance, they are consistently overdone, in a style appropriate to the later Beethoven symphonies.

In the opening bars Solti achieves absolute unanimity of attack on the chords but the result is aggressive rather than noble or grand. When he comes to the second subject in the *Allegro* he maintains the tempo with implacable rigidity. No slowing up is marked at letter B but surely at least a feeling of relaxation is intended, and this is not achieved. The oboe solo sounds rushed and unbending. For all the clarity of Solti's rhythms, at bar 277 the main theme cannot be heard clearly at all in the first violins, basses, celli and bassoons because the rest of the orchestra is so loud.

The second movement is played in much the same way. The first beat of every bar is given a heavy accent, and so too is the eighth-note pick-up whenever it occurs. Within the framework of Solti's inflexible tempo the music sounds like a march. There ought to be suggestions of a march, to be sure, particularly when the timpani joins in with the dotted rhythm later in the movement, however one should not be given the impression that the whole movement *is* a march.

In the last movement the notes are rendered without much humour or excitement. There is little sense of mock drama in the slow introduction, in which the theme of the following *Allegro* is introduced in tantalizing fragments. And when the *Allegro* does begin it is again elephantine when it should be as light as a feather.

My impression is that a powerful and serious personality

has organized and directed this performance. It is tough-minded, stiff and rhythmically exact to a fault. Chords are played like heels clicking together rather than like musical instruments sounding with each other. The result is a reading altogether too tough and severe for the nature of the music — the youthful innocence of the work is lost.

Symphony No. 2 in D major Op. 36

Similar virtues and drawbacks may be found in Solti's performance of the Second Symphony. This is a more ambitious work than the First, but it is still essentially classical in style. It is not a piece given to heaven-storming, let alone even a fleeting glimpse of tragedy, but rather finds its element in a persistent feeling of joy and exuberance. Again, the conductor ought to aim at classical lightness in the textures and articulation in order to facilitate the essential flow of the music. He should also guard against introducing any suggestion of pomposity and aggressiveness. Solti, who encourages his orchestra to play with considerable heaviness, obviously has different ideas about the music. In the *Allegro* section of the first movement, for instance, the notes are hammered flat when they should be released quickly in order to spring forward to the next.

The slow movement is marked *Larghetto* which is surely Beethoven's way of cautioning the conductor not to take the music too slowly. Solti ignores the warning in a performance devoid of grace and buoyancy. As in the First Symphony, he maintains one tempo throughout each movement, even for the *Trio* sections in the *Scherzos* (although the *Scherzo* of the First Symphony is called by the old name, *Menuetto*). While there is no indication in the score that a slower tempo should be taken here, it is traditional to do so — not always a good reason, to be sure, but the music does feel unyielding and hard-driven if there is not at least a slight relaxation in tempo for the *Trios*.

Another unusual feature of Solti's recording of the Second

Symphony is the absence of a single real *pianissimo*. In fact, the first one in the entire cycle does not occur until the beginning of the development section in the first movement of the *Eroica*. It is true that this is an effect Beethoven exploits more fully in his later works, and in no case should the *pianissimo* have the disembodied, dramatic quality essential to fine performances of the Fifth or the Ninth. Nonetheless, there is room for much quieter playing in the Second Symphony at bar 105 in the *Scherzo* and at bar 338 in the last movement, to take just two examples.

Symphony No. 3 in E flat major Op. 55 "Eroica"

Beethoven's Third Symphony is in many respects a new kind of symphony. This is true both of the emotions expressed and of the textures and orchestration — the numbers and kinds of instruments and how they are used — and the two are of course related. On the most superficial level, the *Eroica* is longer and louder, but it is also more wide-ranging in its expression and more complex structurally than either of his first two symphonies. While it can be very effectively played by an orchestra of only medium size, it is not inappropriate to use a larger orchestra. Still, the use of six horns instead of the three called for in the score (a not uncommon occurrence) is going too far. This touch certainly adds to the power of the big climax in the last movement, however, it also pushes Beethoven too far in the direction of Bruckner to be entirely convincing.

Solti's tempo for the first movement is quite moderate. More reminiscent of Klemperer than Toscanini, it is effective at least at the beginning. The heaviness of both sound and accentuation encountered in Solti's performances of the First and Second Symphonies is at last suited to the character of the music. There is tremendous authority through the exposition section, as Solti not only hammers every *sf* but allows the solo winds time to phrase their successive *dolce* entrances. However, doubts about Solti's conception set in when he avoids any sense of climax at bars 275-279. What seems to be required here is a gradual build-up in tension, finally released after it becomes nearly unbearable. In Solti's hands, the sequence is quite uneventful. Further along, at the build-up beginning in the basses and celli (bar 341), the listener is jarred by the strength of the accents when the general marking is *piano*. These overdone *sf*'s are more appropriate to a *forte* passage and their effect here is to destroy a necessary feeling that something ominous is impending. At bar 408 there is an inconsistency between horn and flute concerning the rendering of the repeated quarter notes—the horn plays them *legato*; the flute distinctly separated.

Finally, at the *Coda* of the movement, another instance of Solti's scrupulous adherence to the letter of the score crops up. The trumpets of Beethoven's day did not have available on their instruments all the notes called for in the theme at bar 655, so Beethoven had them begin to play the passage and let the woodwinds finish it alone. Since the modern trumpet can supply all the required notes, it now plays the entire theme in tonic and dominant in most *Eroica* performances—a practice undoubtedly more in line with Beethoven's intentions. To stick slavishly to the score, as Solti does in his Chicago recording, is to do away with the overwhelming grandeur and excitement of this magnificent *Coda*. Solti did follow modern practice in his first *Eroica* with the Vienna Philharmonic, and perhaps he will do so again when he records the work a third time.

The second movement is once more lacking a sure sense of tension and release. It is accurately played but seems episodic and arbitrary. The trumpets surprise us by suddenly bursting forth at bar 96 where we expect to hear the *sempre più f* Beethoven wrote; and where is their power when it is asked for at bar 76? Solti's treatment of the trumpets in such passages is as puzzling as it is unconvincing.

The third movement is played quite fast but, as is so often

the case with Solti, too heavily for the character of the music. The heaviness is here accompanied by a certain nervousness and the result is a tempo that never really settles.

In the last movement, climactic moments go for little, as at bar 381. The music is pushed forward too quickly, and robbed of nobility. In the final *Presto*, the tempo is careful where it should be headlong. The timpani suddenly erupts at bars 457-458 then falls back to nothing. What could Solti have had in mind? There is nothing in the score to justify this strange reading. At bar 469 the brass is held down to about *mf* to allow the clarinets and bassoons to emerge with their scale passages. However, the effect comes across as contrived in the final bars of such a symphony. For the sake of textural clarity the piece finishes with a whimper instead of a bang. Solti is so intent on solving the *Eroica's* technical problems, he utterly fails to give a real performance.

Symphony No. 4 in B flat major Op. 60

"A slender Greek maiden between two giants." Robert Schumann's poetic description of the Fourth Symphony refers to the fact that both the *Eroica* and the Fifth Symphony are much grander in conception, and possess elements of tragedy not to be found in the Fourth. But this is not to say that the B flat is a lesser work; in some ways it is even more beautiful than its neighbours.

Solti's performance with the Chicago Symphony is perhaps the most successful in the entire cycle. Tempos are generally lively and energetic, and not impeded by the rhythmic heaviness prevalent in nearly all of the other performances. Solti seems freer in his approach here and it pays off. The flute solo at bar 304 is customarily slowed down with the basses and cellos, although there is no marking to allow for a *ritardando* in the score. To his credit, Solti follows tradition in this instance and the passage has a lovely effect.

The tempo for the slow movement is a good one — measured, slightly held back, and only occasionally dangerously slow — and the first violins distinguish themselves with playing of great tonal beauty in the opening bars. At letter A and again from bar 50, Solti coaxes a noble sound from his trumpets that is a joy to hear, and gives them a prominence in these passages just sufficient to create dissonances which one will seldom hear brought out so well — a beautifully judged effect.

In the *Scherzo*, Solti goes off the rails several times by being too literal in his approach. His fast tempo is carried straight into the *Trio* each time, even though Beethoven called for *un poco meno allegro*. According to the metronome markings there is to be only a slight difference in tempo, but in Solti's performance there is scarcely any difference at all. And, as happens so often in Solti's Beethoven, the *sforzandi* are greatly overdone at bars 163-166 and again when the same passage is repeated. On the other hand, the last movement is played brilliantly, with first-rate performances by each member of the orchestra. One might regret the consistently loud *pianissimos*, particularly in the basses and cellos at bar 319, but for the most part Solti's energy and alertness pay great dividends here.

Symphony No. 5 in C minor Op. 67

Solti's 1958 recording of the Fifth with the Vienna Philharmonic, while not letter-perfect, is an exciting and bracing performance. Although it is not a subtle reading — the temper often borders on the hysterical — the symphony responds well to such treatment, especially when the orchestra is the Vienna Philharmonic. No matter how fast the tempo, or how loud the volume, the players always produce a rich, beautiful tone where others might sound raucous and crude.

By contrast, Solti's Chicago Fifth is an enormous disappointment. Tempos are much slower and even self-consciously held back. In the first movement, not only is the

"I firmly believe that the essential quality of a conductor is, first of all, that power to project your imagination to other people." — Solti

Solti conducting the Chicago Symphony Chorus and Orchestra in concert at Orchestra Hall.

Solti prepares Carlo Bergonzi and Cornell MacNeil for recording of Verdi's *Un Ballo in Maschera*. Circa 1960. (London Records photo by Eleanor Morrison)

Studio rehearsal of *Un Ballo in Maschera* with the Accademia di Santa Cecilia, Rome, Orchestra. Circa 1960. (London Records photo by Eleanor Morrison)

Stressing a point to the Vienna Philharmonic strings during a 1960 rehearsal of Wagner's *Tristan und Isolde*. (London Records photo)

Carlo Maria Giulini and Solti in the spring of 1971 during Giulini's tenure as Principal Guest Conductor of the Chicago Symphony.

The triumphant return of the Chicago Symphony after its 1971 European tour.

A subdued and thoughtful Solti receives an honorary degree from Oxford University, June 21, 1972.

Playing (and singing) for the incomparable Birgit Nilsson, November 8, 1973.

Solti and Sir Michael Tippett during rehearsals for the premiere of Tippett's Fourth Symphony, October 1977.

"It is his eyes and facial muscles, both of which impart an infectious alertness." From *Solti*.

tempo too slow but the climaxes are greatly underpowered. In an apparent effort to avoid the rhetoric of traditional performances of this movement, Solti goes out of his way to maintain the same tempo throughout, despite the logic of the music. The mighty statements of the main theme by brass and timpani really must be slowed down and each note given progressively more weight coming into the *fermatas* before the oboe solo, and again at the end after bar 475. In this last passage Solti does slow up a little and he does hold the last *fermata* longer than the others; still, it is not enough for a dramatic musical structure on this scale. Moreover, in this same passage, trumpets and timpani must be shattering in their weight and power. Solti, however, keeps them on a very tight rein indeed. The length of the *fermata* is of great importance here too. It must be held long enough to give the impression it will never end, otherwise it is mere repetition without significance. Solti's objective reading is an interesting experiment, perhaps, and Pierre Boulez has made a recording which displays the same kind of detachment, but neither performance should be thought of as idiomatic.

Throughout the second movement the playing is well-controlled. Accompaniment figures emerge with pleasing clarity, and the numerous technical problems are admirably sorted out. But the tempo is too often sluggish to be entirely satisfactory, and once again an excessive self-consiousness intrudes upon the performance. It is almost standard for a conductor playing the music for the first time with a new orchestra to say at the first *forte* in the viola and cello tune (bar 7), "No, no gentlemen, you make a *crescendo* on the E flat when it is *subito forte!*" (See top p. 92)

How clever of the conductor to correct his lazy musicians. Unfortunately, the "lazy musicians," who anticipate the *forte*, usually play the passage with more musicality than Solti achieves from his Chicago orchestra. The *subito forte* is in the score alright, but an interpretation as extreme as Solti's makes no sense at all; it destroys the line. Played so violently, the *subito forte* becomes, in fact, a *sforzando*.

The tempo Solti chooses for the *Finale* is also a little slow. It can be made to work, but not without masterly control of all the tempo changes, and well-judged climaxes at the end, neither of which conditions Solti meets. Failing to reach a climax is a persistent failing in Solti's Beethoven cycle, and as far as the Fifth Symphony is concerned, a reading without an exciting denouement amounts to a gross distortion of the score.

Symphony No. 6 in F major Op. 68 "Pastoral"

The Sixth Symphony is one of the two in the cycle recorded at the Sofiensaal in Vienna. The sound of the orchestra is a great improvement with much more warmth in all sections, and generally far less of the forcing of string tone so common in the Chicago recordings. However, the justly celebrated hall was an unfamiliar one to the players and this, coupled with the fact that the recording was made during a hectic European tour, perhaps account for some of the problems in the performance.

The first two movements go reasonably well but then disaster strikes. In the *Scherzo*, the orchestra is curiously untidy, with the horns in particular being chronically late. It is possible that the horns could not hear the rest of the orchestra well enough, and certainly Solti's very fast tempo does not make things any easier; nevertheless, the playing is disgraceful by any standard. The horns blare out like vicious, barking dogs, while trying desperately throughout the whole movement to catch up with the rest of the orchestra. In the horn solo at the beginning of the last movement, Solti asks for such strange phrasing that the player must have turned himself nearly inside out to manage it. And, once again, there is no majesty in the final climax—in fact, there is scarcely any climax at all.

One can only conclude that time ran out in Vienna before the necessary retakes could be done. This recording should never have been released.

Symphony No. 7 in A major Op. 92

Like the Sixth, Solti's Seventh starts off fine, with a welcome bloom of sound from the Sofiensaal on the opening chords. The second movement is particularly well-played, with beautiful balances in the lower strings.

The third movement is quite fast, even in the *Trio*. Solti follows Toscanini by being true to the letter of the score here — Beethoven has written *assai meno presto* for the *Trio* with a metronome marking indicating one to a bar — still, many conductors believe a much slower tempo makes more sense because it allows the numerous *dolce* hairpins (◁ ▷) to make their effect. In any case, nearly all conductors are sceptical about the accuracy of Beethoven's metronome markings, and judge each one on its merits in the musical context. Solti's fast tempo for the *Trio* in the Seventh may be textually correct, but it sounds rushed and rather messy.

The *Finale* is fast enough without setting a new speed record, though the accents are heavy to the point of sluggishness. Once more Solti holds the orchestra in check at the climax, so that the ending is a considerable let-down.

Symphony No. 8 in F major Op. 93

In conversation with William Mann, Solti observes that the Eighth is probably the easiest Beethoven symphony to conduct but the hardest to play, although no such difficulties seem to exist for the Chicago Symphony. Solti is particularly successful in encouraging his players to articulate every note of every triplet in the last movement. On the other hand, this clarity comes at a price. Surely the passage should be tossed off with a flick of the wrist, yet it would seem Solti worked on the figure to the extent that the players were nearly paralyzed in their bow arms, and so produced a heavier sound without much bounce. The feeling which is exhibited throughout the entire movement is on the ponderous side. At bar 157 one notes that the Chicago Symphony bassoon is no better than his colleagues in most other orchestras in that he fails to play the octaves in tune.

Also in conversation with William Mann, Solti talks about the problem of getting the same kind of *staccato* from all the winds in the opening bars of the second movement. Solti achieves this uniformity, but it is too loud and too heavy; what is needed is a precise and light *staccato*.

The highlight of the recording is the playing of the two horns in the *Trio* of the third movement. The dynamics are beautifully shaped and the sound is out of this world.

Symphony No. 9 in D minor Op. 125 "Choral"

Solti's version of the Ninth, recorded in the Krannert Centre in Chicago, yields a transparency of sound not to be found in either the Medina or the Sofiensaal performances. It is a special pleasure to hear the timpani come through so cleanly and forcefully. For most of the Beethoven recordings the timpani sound is remote and muddy, although this has a good deal to do with Solti's rein on the instrument. In the Ninth, however, the timpani is allowed more prominence. This is particularly important at the recapitulation of the first movement and, of course, in the solo passages in the *Scherzo.*

At the very beginning of the symphony Solti makes the pulse clear in the sextuplet accompaniment while maintaining a true *pianissimo,* and the *sotto voce* entrance of the main theme is perfectly judged. When this same passage is recalled at bar 30 in the *Finale,* one is again struck by how well Solti has captured the serenity of the music. The tempo chosen for the first movement as a whole is moderate, except for a notable episode where Solti dares a much slower pace, with excellent results. At bar 506, and again four bars later, a *ritardando* is indicated followed immediately by the marking *a tempo.* The entire passage is played quite slowly with great expression, and features lovely phrasing by the winds and strings together. Yet, while Solti obeys the *ritardando,* he never really returns to the main tempo of the movement during this episode. Here he ignores Beethoven's markings when the spirit of the music seems to require rather that he obey them.

He also disregards the composer's markings elsewhere in the movement. At bar 194 and at the parallel passage (212), Solti begins the *ritardando* a bar early, but the revision is a very musical one. Another deviation from the score occurs at the recapitulation, where Beethoven has written in *fortissimos* for all instruments, from beginning to end. If the music is played accordingly, it is difficult to make out the return of the main theme in the strings. To allow this figure to emerge, Solti reduces the volume of the accompaniment and makes a *crescendo* toward the thirty-second note attack at the end of bar 304 and again at the end of each bar in which the figure is repeated. (See pp. 96-97)

While this practice is adopted by many conductors and certainly clarifies what is going on in the passage, it is somehow unBeethovenian. When the music is played as written, with all instruments including trumpets and timpani issuing a really powerful *fortissimo* throughout, the melodic figure has to fight to be heard, yet it does come through and the epic grandeur of the passage is matchless. This seems to be what Beethoven intended. Moreover, there is no comparable instance in Beethoven's other works of the *forte-piano crescendo* sequence adopted by Solti. Solti is here retaining a traditional practice favoured by Toscanini and many others, but it bears serious rethinking.

The rest of the symphony is well-played without offering any special insights and, unfortunately, Solti's vocal quartet — Pilar Lorengar, Yvonne Minton, Stuart Burrows and Martti Talvela — is not at all suited to the music. The sound of the individual voices is often ugly and the blend is non-existent. Throughout the performance Solti appears to have given too much thought and attention to technical problems and not enough to the spiritual depths of the score.

Every recording of Solti's Beethoven cycle is a testament to how seriously he regards the technical problems of playing and conducting these works, and in talking with William Mann, Solti refers time and again to such difficulties. It is reassuring for a young conductor to learn that for all his enormous gifts, Solti admits to having trouble beginning the Fifth Symphony and the *Scherzo* of the Third.

Solti has taken great care in these performances to do what he believes to be correct and, in this respect, he has certainly been more deeply influenced by Toscanini's "desperate seriousness," than by Furtwängler's poetic spontaneity. It is obvious that Solti knows what he wants, but his concepts seem only partially developed. One suspects that now he has been able to hear the results of putting his ideas about the entire cycle into practice, he has had second thoughts regarding many points of interpretaiton. Solti possesses the abundance of energy and technique necessary to play the symphonies extremely well. All he lacks is the confidence in his orchestra and in his technique to let the inner qualities of the music emerge. If he continues to work on these symphonies with the Chicago Symphony over a period of years, his second Beethoven cycle might well be much more satisfying.

6
Mahler with Many Orchestras

Solti's recorded Beethoven cycle is the work of a conductor
not quite released from his old self and not fully cognizant of
his new self either. The transitional Solti had trouble
balancing the emotional and the intellectual in Beethoven
because he had not yet found his own equilibrium. The
same observation can be made about Solti's Mahler cycle,
except that Solti was prepared to allow Mahler more excitement and bombast than he thought appropriate in
Beethoven.

The recordings were made over a period of ten years
(1961-1971) and with three different orchestras, so obviously one cannot expect the same unity of style achieved
in the Beethoven cycle. Yet, certain qualities evident
throughout that cycle do persist in the Mahler series. Above
all, there is Solti's rhythmic precision, unequalled by any
conductor at work today, with the possible exception of
Pierre Boulez. Moreover, Solti at his best also has an energy
and drive Boulez lacks. In all Solti's Mahler recordings, and
especially those with the Chicago Symphony, the music is
not so much conducted as propelled forward. Many of his
tempos are extremely fast, but they are never too fast for the
orchestra, nor are they out of control.

Technically and temperamentally, Solti is an excellent
Mahler conductor. He solves the enormous problems of co-
ordinating the huge orchestral and vocal forces and, more
importantly, manages the numerous tempo changes and the
extraordinary dynamic range with great assurance and
conviction. Solti's famous impetuosity, although somewhat
mellowed by the time of these recordings, suits Mahler very
well. The scores contain frequent directions to the con-

ductor to suddenly push forward, and Solti can manage this sort of thing with incomparable energy. Yet the more lyrical and relaxed episodes are handled well too.

Unfortunately, Solti frequently ignores the quiet dynamics in his Mahler performances. Passages which should sound ethereal and mysterious emerge as matter of fact because they are too loud. Perhaps, though, this is an unfair criticism. It is a rare conductor who can encompass Mahler's many moods. And it cannot be stressed often enough what an achievement it is for Solti to cause to be played so many notes so accurately and with such energy. He may fail to bring out the mystical side of the music, but he must be rated as a Mahler conductor of considerable ability nonetheless. It is not an overstatement to say that one has not really heard all the music in these scores unless one has heard them played by Solti and the virtuosos of the Chicago Symphony. Even the celebrated recording of the Fifth Symphony, which Karajan and the Berlin Philharmonic made for DG, does not rival the Chicago Symphony's version in matters of rhythm.

Symphony No. 1 in D major "Titan"

Like all the Mahler symphonies, the First was conceived and has to be understood as a vast organism. At the same time, all the extraordinary and innumerable transformations of the thematic ideas must be given their proper character. The listener should never be in doubt that the music is moving towards a logical and emotionally satisfying conclusion, however that conclusion will be empty if the individuality of each episode has not been experienced along the way. For example, the marches and dances which abound in Mahler's symphonies and which were considered vulgar and cheap before the works were better understood cannot be downplayed or somehow perfumed without sacrificing the rich human experience Mahler was attempting to depict in the language of music. Precisely because they are trite, the marches and dances express an

100

important side of the human experience which co-exists alongside the more elevated and noble qualities of mankind. Similarily, the cruelty and senselessness of war is vividly expressed in Mahler's symphonies, no less so than in Tolstoy's *War and Peace*. But how difficult it is, Mahler is saying, and how necessary to transcend the vulgar and the aggressive and find lasting truth and beauty.

This eternal struggle of the human soul to rise above itself, sometimes finding peace in nature, but ultimately seeking something more lasting in eternal life has to be realized during performance. Conductors must not shrink from the mindlessness and cruelty of Mahler's military marches, just as they must resist the temptation to make the country dances too sophisticated. And they must crown the whole with a blazing belief in Mahler's vision of life everlasting.

The slow introduction to the first movement of the symphony contains the thematic seeds of the whole work, above all, the interval of a descending fourth. It is heard for the first time in the third bar, played softly and in long notes in the minor by the winds, then a little later, played louder and in short notes like a bird call. Further on, the interval is repeated over and over, finally becoming the first two notes of the main theme of the faster section, in a major key version for basses and cellos. At the end of the symphony the interval reappears as part of a triumphal peroration in the major. There is also an important fanfare idea in the slow introduction, first played quietly by the muted trumpets. It too returns brilliantly and triumphantly as part of the climactic outbursts in the *Finale*.

Solti's recording, made in 1964 with the London Symphony, is one of the best in the entire cycle. The orchestra plays superbly and the recording quality is unusually good. Solti masters every mood of the work and conveys a feeling of great involvement. In a BBC interview, also from 1964, Solti recalls that when he first conducted the LSO, in 1952

101

CARL A. RUDISILL LIBRARY
LENOIR RHYNE COLLEGE

or 1953, "it was not terribly good. A few years later Fleischmann became General Secretary and he invited me to come. I was sceptical but it was marvelous. I have great respect for this orchestra. They work very hard to make it better. The string sound has a bite that I like...they can also sing...[a] crisp, clear tone. There are wonderful soloists in the wind group." The London Symphony *had* improved, with the acquisition of outstanding players such as Barry Tuckwell and Gervase de Peyer, but there was also an extraordinary spirit and pride in the group, attributable, at least in part, to the orchestra's self-governing status. The players themselves chose their own colleagues, their manager, their conductors and their engagements. It was certainly Solti's good fortune to make some of his first Mahler recordings with this newly invigorated orchestra.

It is instructive to compare this recording with a later one which Giulini made with Solti's own orchestra, the Chicago Symphony. Giulini takes a consistently lyrical view of the work, often wonderfully expressive, but disappointing in the earthier episodes. His conception seems altogether too elegant for the nature of the music. Solti, on the other hand, is muscular and even crude when need be, and the recording supports this conception with a more striking realization of the different instrumental timbres.

For an indication of how Mahler sought to burst the bonds of traditional orchestral sonority, one need look no further than the composer's instructions to be found on page 163 of the score (Universal Edition). At this point, another set of four horns is added to the seven already in the orchestra and, in addition, all the horns and trumpets are instructed to stand up with their bells raised and to try to drown out everybody else! Never before in orchestral literature had a composer been so explicit and so extravagant in his demands. While this passage can have a tremendous aural and visual effect in the hall, it seldom comes off as well on records where almost any volume increase desired can be achieved simply by turning a knob. The Solti recording is again notably more successful than the Giulini in this section.

Symphony No. 2 in C minor "Resurrection"

The Second Symphony was also recorded with the London Symphony, just two years after the First. If anything, the sound is even better, with a range of dynamics and a depth of perception rivaling the Vienna *Ring* recordings which had been completed only the year before. There are musical resemblances between the Mahler and the Wagner in the score too: the searing string *tremolos* and the attack of the basses and cellos at the beginning of the *Resurrection* are reminiscent of the opening of *Die Walküre* Act I. And in performances of both pieces part of the excitement is the sensation of hearing the physical contact of bow and string, particularly by the double basses. The force of attack Solti coaxes out of the orchestra in the Mahler is staggering. Moreover, he manages to maintain this kind of energy throughout the first movement of the symphony. Only Abbado's 1977 recording of this movement achieves a comparable level of tension and virtuosity.

In the more subdued, even childlike second movement, Solti is equally impressive. The phrasing of the strings is wonderfully varied and subtle, so much so, one could almost mistake the orchestra for the Vienna Philharmonic. The magic continues into the third movement where the tricky interplay between winds and strings is beautifully brought off and at just the right tempo—neither rushed nor self-consciously held back.

The fourth and fifth movements, however, are a great letdown. Trumpets and oboe play with admirable artistry in their quiet moments in the fourth movement, but not nearly softly enough: *pp* is the marking repeatedly. The *molto espressivo* sounds rather cold and the *molto ritenuto* near the end of the movement is surely far too fast. To ignore so many important tempo and dynamic markings is to render this sublime movement commonplace. Soloist Helen Watts contributes little except an accurate reading of the notes.

As Beethoven did in his Ninth Symphony, Mahler introduces a chorus in the final movement of his Second Symphony, and uses it to create an overwhelming effect—the pain and misery of human existence portrayed earlier in the work are superceded at last by resurrection. *"Auferstehen!"* the chorus cries out. "Rise again!" Mahler's music is absolutely gripping and transporting, as it begins softly and mysteriously in the chorus and then bursts forth triumphantly. But time and again in Solti's performance there is a dangerous loss of tension. At the final climax both Solti and the engineers provide only a glimpse of resurrection. It is a musical and carefully prepared performance when, instead, a feeling that the performers have been entirely swept away with the ideas as well as the notes should be engendered. Either Solti was still working towards an understanding of the logic of this part of the score, or he simply failed to get what he wanted under the stop-start conditions of studio recording. What a pity after such an auspicious beginning!

Symphony No. 3 in D minor

Mahler's Third Symphony is a rambling epic with a number of significant musical and philosophical resemblances to the Second Symphony. Both require a chorus and at least one vocal soloist, and both follow a tortuous emotional path towards eternal salvation. The climax in the last movement of the Third recalls the parallel passage in the Second in its triumphal major-key bombast.

Solti's conception of the Third has all the virtues and shortcomings of his performance of the Second: an abundance of energy, great attention to detail, but also a disturbing inability either to comprehend the logic of the whole or to deliver the *coup de grâce*.

It is notoriously difficult for any conductor to hold the long first movement together, but it can be done. Compare, for example, Jascha Horenstein's recording made about the same time and with the same orchestra, the London Symphony. In Solti's hands, the score appears to be a series of unrelated episodes. Horenstein, however, manages to communicate a feeling of integration while still allowing the individual qualities of these episodes their due. Even the seemingly inconsequential drum rolls and trivial tunes have important parts to play in the work as a whole. After letter 11, Horenstein gives the oboe tune a character missed entirely by Solti, yet absolutely faithful to Mahler's markings in the score.

In the last movement, Solti takes too fast a tempo at letter 26, in the passage marked *sehr langsam*. Again, he fails to get inside the music. This is a characteristic and heart-rending sequence for three trumpets and trombone. There is a risk that the music might fall apart if taken too slowly here, and Horenstein's brass players do have trouble with both breath control and intonation, but so do Solti's (the very same players?) at a faster tempo. James Levine and the Chicago Symphony achieve much better results on their recording, and with a tempo as slow as Horenstein's.

Symphony No. 4 in G major "Ode to Heavenly Joy"

The G major is the first Mahler symphony Solti recorded, and at that time (1961) there was no suggestion he would go on to record all nine. The Concertgebouw, Solti's orchestra for this production, was certainly no stranger to the Fourth. Its first performance of the work was in 1904, just three years after the premiere. The composer himself was on the podium and, in fact, conducted the symphony twice at the same concert! Willem Mengelberg, the orchestra's Music Director, conducted the work a year later and many times thereafter, most notably in his Mahler Festival of 1921 and in a 1939 recorded performance. Mengelberg and the

Concertgebouw were steeped in Mahler and the style and spirit of his music. It is appropriate that Mengelberg's successors, Eduard Van Beinum and Bernard Haitink, have also shown an affinity for Mahler, and that both have recorded the Fourth Symphony with the orchestra. Solti's version made for four recordings over about a thirty-year period of the same work by the same orchestra.

In spite of the fact that the Concertgebouw learned its Mahler from the composer himself, and that the score is meticulously marked with all sorts of detailed instructions concerning tempo and dynamics, the four performances are by no means identical. Mengelberg, of course, had a reputation for being a wilful, eccentric conductor. His interpretations were both daringly unique and controversial, but there was no disputing his control over the orchestra, nor the inspired quality of his best performances. The singularity of his style can be heard in his 1939 recording of the Fourth, which is in very good sound and readily available today. In the first movement in the third bar there is a marking *un poco ritardando*. When the same figure is repeated fourteen bars later there is no such marking, and no other conductor slows up at this point except Mengelberg. Later in the movement, at letter 7, Mengelberg adds another of his inimitable touches, stretching out the top note of the the phrase each time. Although Mahler did mark an accent on these notes, Mengelberg's interpretation virtually amounts to a rewriting of the rhythm.

106

Mahler's Fourth is his least ambitious symphony. The orchestration is almost classical in its modest requirements of two trumpets and no trombones, and there is no heaven-storming, apocalyptic *Finale*. On the contrary, the symphony ends quietly. Nonetheless, there are some highly original touches. In the second movement, for example, the concertmaster must use two instruments tuned differently—one a whole tone higher than the other—to suggest the brazen, rather coarse playing of a street fiddler.

In the last movement there are surprising disagreements among conductors about the proper tempo. Bruno Walter, Mahler's associate for many years and one of the foremost interpreters of his music, took quite a fast tempo. Mengelberg, with an equal claim to know the composer's intentions, conducted the movement far more slowly. Solti decided on a middle course.

Solti's performance, as a whole, is technically superb, with some characteristically rich and exciting playing by members of the Concertgebouw. The recording quality is excellent too. All that is lacking is that otherworldly beauty which is so necessary in the last two movements. Mengelberg achieves it, and so too does Haitink with the help of the finest soprano to grace any recording of the Mahler Fourth: Elly Ameling. Solti's soloist is the competent but rather ordinary Sylvia Stahlman.

Symphony No. 5 in C sharp minor

This 1970 recording is the first in Solti's Mahler series to be made with his own orchestra, the Chicago Symphony. While the orchestral playing throughout the cycle is first-rate, on the Chicago Symphony recordings it is superb. One generally assumes, and makes allowances for the fact, that brass instruments lack the agility of winds or strings. The Mahler symphonies are filled with tough passages for brass which require not only agility, but security and strength in the upper registers, as well as the stamina to sustain such difficult playing over the course of works lasting up to ninety minutes. Of course stamina is not a problem in a recording. If the players should tire, the piece can be finished the next day; or, the strenuous passages can be scheduled early in the session. Also, to some extent, additional strength can be supplied by the engineer. Even so, the brass, and indeed all the instrumentalists in the Chicago Symphony recordings are astounding.

As was mentioned earlier in the chapter, Solti and his Chicago players often surpass Karajan and the Berlin Philharmonic in their respective recordings of the Mahler Fifth. Both performances are tremendously powerful in the opening bars of the first and second movements, although Solti's brass is more accurate. On the other hand, Karajan and his strings achieve a more poetic sound at letter 2 in the first movement, and again before letter 12. Solti's *Finale*, however, sets new standards of performance for this movement. He takes an exhilaratingly fast tempo, and yet his horns produce a *staccatissimo* that makes their Berlin counterparts sound sloppy in comparison. And listen to the cellos at letter 2! They far outshine the Berliners in their playing of the *staccato* eighth notes. Overall, Solti's realization brings out more of the humour obviously intended by Mahler with his *allegro giocoso* marking.

The moments one regrets in Solti's reading are few. In the quiet passages, before letter 9 and after letter 27, where Karajan produces a fine inward quality, Solti's sound is too loud. And at the big climax after letter 33, Solti's trumpets almost disappear when, as in Karajan's recording, they should blare forth triumphantly.

Symphony No. 6 in A minor "Tragic"

Solti's recording of the Sixth Symphony, also with the Chicago Symphony, is another virtuosic *tour de force*. His conducting is super-aggressive and dynamic, and the orchestra produces some incredibly fast, loud playing. But again, while this approach suits the music most of the time, one misses some of the tenderness and ethereal softness heard in other versions.

Solti's tempo for the first movement is arguably at odds with the *allegro energico ma non troppo* called for in the score. His fast beginning is impressive until letter 7 which, according to Mahler's instructions, is supposed to be played at the same tempo. The theme here is softer, more expressive and more lyrical. Solti's quick tempo causes it to sound superficial rather than hauntingly beautiful.

The *Finale* contains the most remarkable playing in the entire Mahler cycle. After letter 33, strings, woodwinds and brass alike play their rapid sixteenths with equal agility and with absolute fearlessness, as if technical problems did not exist. And at Solti's ferocious tempo, it is all quite breathtaking.

Symphony No. 7 in E minor "Song of the Night"

This too is a Chicago Symphony performance, and is surely the finest Mahler Seventh yet put on records. In comparison, the others seem hopelessly underrehearsed and incoherent. The most original movement is the third, with its almost Webernesque melodies, irregular rhythms, and odd orchestration. The rhythm settles into waltz time but it is a demented waltz — a waltz for a society coming apart at the seams, haunted by its own inadequacy and guilt. Solti brings out this nightmarish quality with great assurance.

An important element in his conducting here is the incisive accenting. Only by stressing every accent can Mahler's unusual rhythmic patterns make their full effect, and Solti gives the music exactly what is needed. This relentless accenting has always been a part of Solti's conducting style, although it has not always been a virtue. The accents in his recording of Wagner's *Tristan und Isolde* are so unremitting, one begins to feel a little seasick after a while. In Mahler, however, where there are often three of four rhythmic patterns going on simultaneously and where the music can so easily become porridge, with neither shape nor clarity of texture, Solti's approach is a great advantage.

Sharp accenting also does wonders for the notoriously problematic last movement of the Seventh, with its frequent complex fugal passages and its tricky alternation of two main tempos. While Solti takes the second tempo (two bars before letter 234) correctly in terms of Mahler's instructions regarding the relation between the two tempos, it appears to be too fast. He has to slow up a little later on, and quite drastically at the *pesante* passage after letter 237. This trouble shifting gears occurs in a number of places throughout the movement, but the rhythmic life and energy in Solti's conducting are major compensations. He brings more cogency to the music than any other conductor on record. The sound is exemplary, save for the usual lack of truly quiet passages, and the balances are good too except that, as in the recording of the Fifth, the trumpets are consistently cut back in favour of the horns. The Chicago Symphony horn players are spectacularly good; still, that does not mean they should be heard at the expense of the trumpets.

Symphony No. 8 in E flat major "The Symphony of a Thousand"

The Eighth was the last of Solti's Mahler cycle to be completed, and it was done under rather unusual circumstances. The original plan had been to record the work in Chicago with the magnificent Chicago Symphony Chorus. Unfortunately, it was discovered that the choristers would have to be paid staggering fees, and a cheaper scheme was therefore proposed. The Chicago Symphony was touring Europe in 1971 — why not arrange for it to stop over in Vienna and make use of one of Europe's best choirs, the Vienna Singverein? In effect, it was much cheaper to send the orchestra to Europe than to record the work at home in Chicago! For Solti it must have been especially attractive to return to the scene of past glories — where the highly-acclaimed *Ring* cycle had been recorded — this time with his own orchestra.

Solti's performance contains plenty of his usual energy, but he manages some calm and inward moments as well, particularly at *Alles Vergängliche* (All things transitory) in the final section. Also on the plus side in this recording is the presence of several fine soloists (tenor René Kollo as Doctor Marianus and Heather Harper as Magna Peccatrix). And Solti deserves enormous credit for mustering such a robust sound from the Singverein, especially when it is evident that this is not really his kind of choir. He seems to be striving to achieve what he already had in the Chicago Symphony Chorus: a choral ensemble with as much technical virtuosity as his orchestra.

The most serious drawback in the recording is the quality of sound. For a conductor and company with such a incomparable *Ring* cycle to their credit, it is a major disappointment. Part of the trouble may have been due to the lack of rehearsal time, which is always a problem under touring conditions. How else to account for the numerous rough and obvious edits? How else to make sense of the general lack of clarity of the sound? At the end of the symphony the extra brass make a considerable effect, but still come nowhere near to equalling the weight and quality of sound produced by the Vienna Philharmonic in the *Ring*. Admittedly, the basic sound of Chicago Symphony is different from that of the Vienna Philharmonic. Nonetheless, as a production job, this recording simply cannot be seriously considered alongside the *Ring* achievement. To make matters worse, tenor René Kollo is off-mike virtually throughout the whole first movement, but then much of his part was dubbed in later because of illness and scheduling problems.

Symphony No. 9 in D major

To turn from Solti's flawed recording of the Mahler Eighth to his brilliant recording of the Ninth made in London four years earlier, is to be able to reaffirm the conductor's great qualities as a Mahler interpreter. Compare it to the almost universally-acclaimed 1976 recording of the work by Giulini and the Chicago Symphony for DG, and it is just as rich and detailed, but even more vivid. Surprisingly though, considering the Chicago Symphony is supposed to be unrivaled, especially in the Mahler repertoire, there is not much to choose between the orchestras. In a work with so many horn solos, the quality of the principal horn player can make a big difference, and while both players are superlative, there is something extra provided by the LSO's musician (Barry Tuckwell?). In addition to remarkable technical feats and thrilling power, he produces a rare expressive quality. Solo oboe and violin have their special moments too in the Solti recording.

Solti's Mahler Ninth is full of muscle and, for some, might be too aggressive. If one compares Solti and Giulini in the third movement, for example, and is partial to Solti, his drive and rhythmic energy, above all in the hair-raising final *più stretto* and *presto*, will make Giulini appear casual to the point of sloppiness, and absurdly elegant. On the other hand, Giulini supporters will charge Solti with being brutal and insensitive. His relentless *staccato* will seem monotonous to listeners sympathetic to Giulini's more musical kind of articulation. Furthermore, Solti will appear to miss entirely the right feeling for the middle section after letter 36, even though he obeys the letter of the score in not slowing up. Giulini does achieve an undeniably remarkable quiet beauty in this passage, and it is this kind of revelatory interpretative touch, Giulini's admirers insist, which demonstrates precisely what Solti's conducting lacks: only rarely can he make the imaginative leap from the page of a score to the mind of the composer. Solti's opponents grant that his work is technically of the highest order, but they feel it lacks distinction. This is a thorny argument at best and will be considered at length in a later chapter. Suffice it to say here that Solti, in his own way, interprets the music as much as

Giulini.

Solti does not charge through the score of the Mahler Ninth all guns blazing, as one might be led into believing from the above. The sheer physical excitement and weight of his reading are striking, but other qualities emerge too. The closing pages of the first movement are chamber music, and Solti plays them that way. There is no pushing or pulling here, no larger-than-life accents. The tonal beauty of the two horns, oboe and solo violin is one of the glories of this performance. The climax of the last movement (Universal Edition, p. 176) is perfectly judged with respect to both tempo and dynamics. In comparison, Giulini's climax is rather ordinary.

Solti also manages most of the tempo contrasts in the second movement with admirable adroitness. His initial tempo is quite slow yet very rhythmic. It makes even more sense at the *poco più mosso subito* (Tempo II), because this section need not go really quickly to sound lively. Solti throttles back with great aplomb for the slow and expressive *ländler* (Tempo III), but he does err thirteen bars later in taking the return of Tempo I so fast. Perhaps he forgot his initial slow tempo. Later still, the extremely long *luftpause* before the return of Tempo III (Universal Edition, p. 84) is a questionable touch.

Still, these are relatively minor quibbles within the context of such an exciting and committed performance. Both conductor and orchestra convey a joy of music-making, and the engineers have captured it all in spectacular sound.

Das Lied von der Erde "*The Song of the Earth*"

This song cycle or symphony with two solo voices belongs, as does the Ninth Symphony, to the last period of Mahler's life. Both works reflect the composer's awareness of his own impending death and his preoccupation with its meaning. He did not live to hear either work performed.

For his texts, Mahler chose some Chinese poems which had been recently translated and which perfectly reflected his mood. Each of the poems combines images of joy, usually in nature, with bittersweet visions of death. The basic theme of *The Song of the Earth* is the ephemeral nature of both life and beauty, and the imminence of death. The first of the six songs in the cycle, for example, includes the lines:

The heavens are ever blue, but you, man how long will you live? Not a hundred years. So take up the wine — dark is life, dark is death.

The symphony therefore begins with an almost demented attempt to live life to the full in the face of its obvious brevity. To perform the first movement, both tenor and orchestra must capture this reckless mood of merry-making. The music should be tossed off with abandon, and almost violent in its passion. Mahler has certainly called for this in the score, with the poor tenor in danger of being overwhelmed by the orchestra on every page. But the performers must also be sensitive to the quieter, more lyrical pages of the song which are full of characteristically Mahlerian sentiment.

Solti's tenor in this performance, René Kollo, has recorded the work no less than three times already in his young career: first with Solti in 1972, then with Bernstein during the same year, and most recently with Karajan in 1975. The three recordings indicate considerable development on Kollo's part, but also reveal the different approaches of the conductors. Solti is, as one might expect, the most aggressive. His orchestra plays louder, the accents are sharper and, in general, the tempos are faster.

There is also a difference in recording quality. Solti's engineers prefer to spotlight instruments, as do Columbia's for Bernstein, whereas their DG counterparts opt for a more natural blend of sound for Karajan. Spotlighting is not necessarily unsuitable in Mahler, but what is unacceptable is the balance between soloists and orchestra. In Solti's recording both Kollo and Yvonne Minton are too often submerged, and while this is not unlike what one might hear in concert, it is inexcusable in a recording. Here is one way in which studio production can improve on concert hall realism.

This choice of balance on Solti's recording destroys an otherwise fine performance. Within DG's ambience, Karajan and Kollo bring out some uncommonly beautiful quiet and lyrical moments of the score, and Kollo's voice floats more freely. Still, one does miss the earthiness of Solti's conception, so vital to the opening song. Bernstein tends towards the Karajan approach, perhaps because his orchestra, the Israel Philharmonic, has a more mellow, less aggressive sound.

In the final *Abschied*, Karajan's blended sound becomes more of a liability than a virtue. Strangely, for him, he seems unable to sustain such a long and subdued slow movement. Solti is better here thanks to crisper accenting and a more detailed sound quality. But Bernstein is best of all in his unfailing concentration and his command of mood and line. Solti is also handicapped by a competent but far from memorable performance of the solo part by Yvonne Minton. Christa Ludwig does a much finer job for Karajan and, perhaps because it is a live performance, excels even more in the Bernstein recording.

Lovers of Mahler's music will know that, in addition to *Das Lied von der Erde*, he began a Tenth Symphony. He finished the first movement and left extensive sketches for the rest of the work from which musicologist Deryck Cooke produced a fully orchestrated performing version. Many conductors have played it and a couple have also recorded it—Eugene Ormandy has recorded Cooke's first version, and Wynn Morris followed Cooke's revised edition. Many more conductors have been reluctant to accept Cooke's work as an authentic Mahler symphony, and they therefore perform only the first movement. Solti has praised Cooke's version. In a 1967 BBC interview he said, "I was shocked. I think it's a marvelous piece of music. It leads so clearly to twentieth century language, to Schönberg and Stravinsky." But Solti has not recorded either Cooke's complete version or Mahler's first movement.

Solti's Mahler cycle is a remarkably distinguished one. Among the conductors who have recorded all the symphonies—Kubelik, Bernstein, Haitink and Abravanel —Solti must be regarded as one of the most successful. His major contribution has been to show how well much of this music can be played. It is not so long ago that even dedicated Mahlerians complained that certain passages could never be made to "sound," or that the brass or string writing was awkward. With both the Chicago Symphony and the London Symphony Solti has put an end to this sort of talk once and for all. Moreover, he has demonstrated that Mahler's music can be made to sound like orchestral showpieces. This is really a considerable achievement. His readings may be lacking in mystery as a result, but then no conductor has ever succeeded in encompassing all the riches of both music and ideas in these works, and perhaps none ever will.

7
The Interpreter in the Opera House

Solti's involvement with opera goes back to the very beginning of his career in Budapest, and continues today with appearances at Covent Garden, the Paris Opera, the Vienna Staatsoper and La Scala.

When he left the Royal Opera House in 1971, Solti planned to spend most of his time henceforth on the concert platform and, for the most part, he has stuck to that position while setting aside several months each year for opera. But at one point, it appeared as if he had changed his mind. Within two years of his departure from Covent Garden he accepted the post of Musical Advisor to the Paris Opera. He seemed to be plunging back into all the plotting and turmoil of a major opera house, although he did not see his decision in that light:

> Liebermann asked me to do it and I wanted to give him the credit of my name. So I worked out a programme for his first two seasons. But he and I knew this was just to get over the first hurdle. I am a guest conductor, like any other. (*Opera News*, September 1976)

Rolf Liebermann had performed miracles as Intendant of the Hamburg Opera and, with Solti's help, believed he could do the same with the Paris Opera. The house had been a notorious basket case for years, with poor management, slack discipline in the orchestra and mostly dismal performances. The French government made a policy decision that the Paris Opera was, in fact, one of the bastions of French culture and must be brought up to international standards. Sufficient funds were made available and the best administrator around — Liebermann — was hired to get things moving. Liebermann knew that firm and experienced musical direction was essential in a major opera

117

house, and so he turned immediately to Solti whose success in building the musical side of the company at Covent Garden paralleled Liebermann's building programme in Hamburg. The two would make an unbeatable team of opera directors.

Solti willingly responded to the plea for help from his old and respected friend, and he was no doubt flattered to be called in on such a prestigious project. At the same time, as he himself has pointed out, he agreed to make only guest appearances as a conductor. During the years of his involvement with the Paris Opera he just managed to live up to this commitment, rarely conducting more than one opera each season. He first mounted the podium for Mozart's *Marriage of Figaro* which opened in the spring of 1973. A performance symbolic of the new era of French culture, it was given in Louis XV's Opera Royal at Versailles before an invited audience of 750 guests paying between $200 and $500 each. The production was later moved to the Paris Opera's own house. In the fall of that same year, Solti returned to lead the first performances in France of Schönberg's *Moses und Aron,* one of his great triumphs at Covent Garden. For the Paris Opera, the work was done in French with Raymond Gerome producing and also taking the part of Moses. Richard Lewis was Aron, as he had been for Solti in London. Solti again emerged triumphant:

> Solti's precise, vital direction was everything one could wish for, in turns mysterious, frenzied, triumphant, and the chorus sang magnificently. Surely every recording company must now have its eyes fixed on the Paris Opera Orchestra and Chorus. (Charles Pitt, *Opera,* December 1973)

In successive years Solti returned to Paris to conduct *Don Giovanni* and *Otello,* and both were well-received. Overall, under Liebermann and Solti, the Paris Opera was raised to world-class stature with amazing rapidity. And to ensure that this achievement received due attention, the company took to the road. In the fall of 1976 it sent an orchestra of 104 and a chorus of 100 to Washington, D.C. and New

York. Billed as the French contribution to the American Bicentennial celebrations, the troupe performed three operas: *Marriage of Figaro, Otello* and *Faust.* Each one featured first-class soloists on the order of Edith Mathis, Frederica von Stade and Tom Krause in *Figaro,* Margaret Price and Carlos Cossutta in *Otello* and Mirella Freni and Nicolai Gedda in *Faust*; and each involved stagings which were also far from routine. Max Bignen's iron and crystal sets for *Faust* were highly original. So too were Svoboda's stark white blocks for *Otello.* And Giorgio Strehler brought out an unusual degree of social and political commentary in his direction of *Figaro.*

Solti was in the pit for *Figaro* and *Otello,* and his firm hand was an important contribution to the success of both productions. Unfortunately, the Met in New York is much too large for *Figaro,* and the fine points in the performance went undetected. The unexpected unevenness of the singing was a further misfortune — while von Stade stopped the show as Cherubino, Christiane Eda-Pierre proved a positive embarrassment as the Countess.

Otello was much more successful, with a solid cast and a scale of orchestral sound more appropriate to the house. It is some indication of the former state of artistic direction at the Paris Opera that this work, which is unquestionably one of the masterpieces of the repertoire, had not been produced at the house since 1894. Its long overdue revival had premiered earlier in the year in Paris, where it was enthusiastically received:

> Sir Georg Solti, as one might expect, drew everything together tautly. He is, in addition, learning to relax, to give the lyrical music its head. Not only did he produce effects of remarkable brilliance in places like the opening storm and the Act III *Finale,* he also, for the first time in my experience, got close to the poetical tenderness of the love duet, and to the poignancy of the Quartet in Act II. (Dale Harris, *Music and Musicians,* September 1976)

In New York, the critics were rapturous in their praise. Solti is something of a cult figure in the city anyway;

however his intense, vibrant conducting was deserving of the accolades.

Nineteen seventy-six was undoubtedly the year of Solti's deepest involvement with the Paris Opera. Not only did he prepare *Otello* in July and then take it to the United States along with *Figaro,* he embarked, near the end of the year, on preparations for a new *Ring* cycle. Ingmar Bergman was announced as producer, but for some reason backed out of the project. In his place, Peter Stein directed *Rheingold* and Klaus Michael Grüber took charge of *Walküre.* Solti conducted performances of both works in December of 1976. Then he too withdrew. His opera conducting in Paris has since slackened off considerably, and his energies in this area are now devoted more to Covent Garden.

Solti loves opera, yet will only do it these days under the best conditions. He does not want to be involved in administrative problems any more, feeling that time spent in such activities takes away from creative work. So, of all the tempting offers that come his way, he usually selects only one each year that will both challenge him and allow him to achieve the highest possible standards. One such project will be a *Die Meistersinger* at La Scala in 1980.

On records, as in the opera house, Solti's repertoire is very heavily weighted in favour of Wagner. Since there are many who regard him as the finest living Wagner conductor, it is not surprising that Decca should think it important to document his work and, in fact, has done so to the extent that Solti has recorded more complete Wagner operas than any other conductor in history. Of the mature works only *Lohengrin* remains to be done.

Tristan und Isolde was recorded in 1960, two years after *Rheingold* and before the other three parts of the *Ring,* and the production made use of many of the Tetralogy's participants. John Culshaw was the producer, the orchestra was the Vienna Philharmonic, and Birgit Nilsson—the *Ring* cycle Brünnhilde—played Isolde. As part of its boxed set of the complete opera, Decca included a record of rehearsal excerpts. While it was intended primarily as a glimpse behind the scenes of how a complex recording is made, it also offers a revealing portrait of Solti in action. The man's enormous energy and involvement are apparent throughout, whether rehearsing the singers with piano, discussing the recording set-up with Culshaw, or rehearsing the orchestra. Unfortunately, the performance is overwrought: climaxes are exciting but frequently noisy and vulgar; accents are too often overdone, destroying line and proportion; and the quieter moments lack tenderness. This recording is valuable mainly as a document of Nilsson's Isolde. Although her interpretation of character and text is uninteresting, when she rears back and lets fly she produces a volume of glorious sound the like of which one might only dream of ever hearing from another Isolde. Poor Fritz Uhl as Tristan is overwhelmed by her, in addition to being mercilessly hammered by Solti.

All but one of the Solti's Wagner opera recordings have been made with the Vienna Philharmonic, an orchestra which plays gloriously under almost any circumstances, except for a tendency to be lax in matters of precision. Traditionally, the ensemble is not interested in the hair-trigger precision of American orchestras and, at times, Solti seems to be trying to force a rhythmic accuracy onto the orchestra. He may find the effort frustrating, but his perserverance is usually rewarded by a much tighter sound. For its part, the orchestra lends to the performances its famous warmth and poetry—qualities Solti's conducting usually lacks, but which the Vienna Philharmonic radiates no matter who is on the podium. The result is that conductor and players complement each other wonderfully. Throughout most of the *Ring, Tannhäuser, Parsifal* and *Die Meistersinger,* the beauty of the orchestral playing is something to marvel at.

The one opera recorded outside Vienna is the *Flying Dutchman,* with the Chicago Symphony. It is a precise, alert performance, more to be respected than enjoyed. The American orchestra does not play badly—far from it—however, after years of getting used to the "Solti-Vienna sound," I am disappointed. This *Dutchman* recording is very revealing of Solti as a Wagner conductor. Without the Vienna Philharmonic he is apt to be square and superficial. The precision of ensemble in Chicago is not mitigated and softened by the natural *espressivo* of the Vienna strings. Further comparisons are possible since Solti has also recorded the *Meistersinger Prelude* with the Chicago Symphony (1972), and the complete opera including the *Overture* with the Vienna Philharmonic (1975). In the Chicago recording the horn parts are so prominent the work could be mistaken for a concerto for four horns. The accents and articulation are such that this noble music takes on the character of a military march. While this *is* processional music, it is intended within the context of the opera to be festive, not military. In the Vienna performance the feeling is quite different. The accents are not quite so heavy, the horns are not blasting so much and the spirit is more appropriate.

Of Solti's other Wagner recordings, *Tannhäuser* and *Parsifal* provide the best quality of sound. Not only is it spectacular, in the tradition of Decca's *Ring* cycle, it is several degrees more natural. René Kollo's refreshingly youthful heldentenor sound graces both recordings, and Helga Dernesch as Elisabeth in *Tannhäuser,* although not as magnificent on the high notes as Nilsson might have been, is very effective in the quieter passages. She makes Elisabeth an understandable object of the affections of both Wolfram and Tannhäuser.

The *Parsifal* recording is consistently excellent and is probably Solti's finest Wagner conducting on records. The *Prelude* lacks a little tension but nearly everything else is glowing and organically conceived in ways quite alien to the Solti of former years. As compared with the competition, Solti's *Parsifal* is unparalleled. It is also the only studio-made recording available. The earlier Knappertsbusch version from Bayreuth has certain special qualities characteristic of that conductor at his best; however his later version suffers from dull sound. The most recent live recording from Bayreuth, with Pierre Boulez conducting, is simply a travesty. Boulez apparently set out to demonstrate how empty Wagner could be, and succeeded. For all his legendary comprehension of twentieth century music, Boulez seems incapable of dealing with the nineteenth century repertoire on its own terms.

Given the considerable problems of casting each of the Wagner operas—there are rarely ideal singers available all at the same time for each role and, if there are, contractual difficulties invariably arise because an artist is exclusively bound to another record company—Decca has maintained an extremely high standard in its Wagner series. Solti, too, has amply repaid the confidence shown in him back in the late 1950's by the Decca management. Except for the *Tristan* debacle, he has conducted a strong series of performances from *Das Rheingold* through *Parsifal*. No other conductor has ever had the opportunity to record so many Wagner works, but it would be difficult to suggest one who might have done them better.

Solti's recordings do have their weaknesses, of course—it would be amazing if such a prolific, ambitious output were free of them—and they are especially apparent in *Die Meistersinger*. One of the major liabilities is Norman Bailey as Hans Sachs. This fine singer and actor was well below his best when the recording was made, and it is an unhappy experience to hear him barking and straining. René Kollo is very good as Walther, as he is on Karajan's EMI recording which was made previously in Dresden, but the rest of the cast is little more than adequate. Solti seems to be less incisive than usual, although the opera does not really allow for massive outbursts on the scale of the *Ring* music dramas. The more mature Solti at least knows that he cannot force the sound the way he was apt to do in the *Tristan* recording;

nonetheless, his restraint is not accompanied by any ability to bring out the poetry of the score. Compare Karajan on almost any page to hear what more careful attention to dynamics or phasing can do. Jochum, in his *Die Meistersinger* recording, is also much more satisfying than Solti.

Solti enjoys the distinction of having recorded more Richard Strauss than any other conductor, with the exception of Karl Böhm. However, as far as circumstances for recording are concerned, Solti has come out ahead of his rival. He has done all his operatic Strauss with the Vienna Philharmonic, whereas Böhm has had to make do with orchestras of lesser stature. And while Böhm was stuck with a fading Inge Borkh for *Electra* and an inadequate Gwyneth Jones for *Salome,* Solti was blessed with Birgit Nilsson in her prime for both works.

The first of Solti's Strauss recordings was *Arabella,* and it remains the only complete recording of the work in the catalogue. Although the sound is not ideal, nearly everything else is, including Lisa Della Casa (in glorious voice) and George London as the protaganists. Solti followed *Arabella* with *Salome, Electra, Der Rosenkavalier,* and *Ariadne auf Naxos.* While each recording has a strong cast and great moments, *Electra* is the most outstanding. Solti's high-strung temperament is ideal for such a score. There is tremendous tension and sweep in his conducting here, with hair-raising playing by the Vienna Philharmonic. And there is love and relaxation too as, for example, after the recognition of Orest.

Early in his career Solti was categorized as a conductor of German opera. This is not surprising, considering his recorded *Ring* cycle and the continuous stream of excellent Wagner and Strauss discs. Still, Solti has worked hard to combat this type-casting by spending a significant portion of his time on Verdi and Mozart. Over the years he has conducted most of the major works of both composers. To date, he has recorded six Verdi and two Mozart operas. The surprising exceptions are Mozart's *Marriage of Figaro,* which Solti has conducted so often it has almost become a calling-card, and Verdi's *La Traviata* and *Il Trovatore.* But the most notable gap in Solti's operatic repertoire is Puccini—he has recorded only a single work (*La Bohème*) by the Italian composer. Nor has he given much attention to Puccini in the opera house. Of all the operas Solti conducted at Covent Garden only one was by Puccini, and that was the one-acter *Gianni Schicchi.* For a conductor with generally broad tastes, Solti's aversion to Puccini is rather puzzling. There are other conductors who probably could do more for *Bohème* or *Butterfly,* but *Tosca* seems to be just right for Solti.

Solti's Verdi recordings have been deservedly overshadowed by his Wagner and Strauss. The latter were nearly all made under optimum conditions in Vienna, with the best singers and producers, and with the continuity necessary for consistently high standards. By contrast, only one of the Verdi operas was recorded in Vienna: a documentation of the *Otello* production prepared for the Paris Opera in 1977. The cast is nearly identical, but the Vienna Philharmonic instead of the Paris Opera Orchestra, is a distinct improvement. Carlos Cossutta does not give us a character study to be classed with Vickers, nor is his voice up there with the great ones; yet this recording, which is the most recent and probably the best of Solti's Verdi on disc, is still an exciting and vivid one.

Solti's earlier Verdi recordings were made, for the most part, in Rome, with ordinary orchestras and ill-chosen casts. Solti deserves a great deal of credit for encouraging his orchestras to play so alertly and so accurately in these performances—there are some thrilling moments in each one of them—however, the Italian orchestras tend to sound raw and vulgar, and the younger Solti had rather too much of these qualities himself. The combination produces some exceedingly unpleasant episodes in *Falstaff,* redeemed only

in part by Solti's unflagging energy. This recording at least
has a strong cast headed by Geraint Evans and Giulietta
Simionato with Mirella Freni and Alfredo Kraus as a fresh-
sounding pair of lovers. But what can one say in defense of
Rigoletto with Robert Merrill walking through the title role
and Anna Moffo scooping and swooning? — overall, it is a
performance lacking in the essential ingredients of menace
and mystery. This is also true of *Aïda,* although both
Leontyne Price and Jon Vickers offer tremendously
powerful characterizations.

Verdi's *Don Carlos* was recorded in London with forces
drawn from the Royal Opera House and, in this respect, was
an important milestone indicating the new status of the
house under Solti. When he arrived it would not have oc-
cured to anyone to record a Royal Opera production for
commercial distribution. Thanks to Solti's initiative and the
fine work of his successor Colin Davis, this is a commonplace
practice at Covent Garden today. Admittedly, the orchestra
is not the Vienna Philharmonic and the sound Decca
achieves for *Don Carlos* is far inferior to the Vienna
recordings, but a unified conception emerges containing
some fine performances by Renata Tebaldi, Grace Bumbry,
Carlo Bergonzi and Nicolai Ghiaurov. Solti is curiously
subdued, particularly in the more spectacular scenes where
some of the old fire would be welcome.

Solti did not conduct any Verdi at all until after the war.
Since that time, though, he has regularly conducted most of
the works of the composer's maturity, and rarely with
anything less than great competence. We are still waiting,
however, for anything to compare with the best of the
Wagner and Strauss series. As a further indication of the
seriousness with which Solti approaches Verdi — as if any
were really needed aside from his performances — an article
Solti wrote for *Opera News* in December 1963 called "The
Verdi I Know" is well worth reading. This essay, which is
part-autobiographical and part-analytical, demonstrates
genuine insight into the distinctive requirements of each of

Verdi's operas. Solti also adds a thoughtful comment about the composer's choice of keys:

> I think that too little importance is attributed to Verdi's key relationships. In *Don Carlos* the dark keys predominate—F sharp minor, C sharp minor—reflecting the mood of the Spanish world. Verdi did not use them frequently in other operas. *Aïda,* on the other hand, is all B flat major, E flat major, and even the minor keys have brighter colours: F minor, E flat minor, B flat minor. It is hard to describe music and its effects, but choice of key does create atmosphere.

Mozart is another of the composers to whom Solti has felt drawn throughout his career, but his performances of the composer's operas, live or on record, are nowhere near his most successful. One of Solti's greatest assets is his ability to extract the maximum rhythmic clarity from any scores he conducts, and one of his most serious deficiencies is his tendency towards heavy accentuation. The combination of these qualities is fatal in Mozart, where rhythmic clarity must be coupled with lightness. Solti's Mozart moves, but more as a result of the application of external pressure than because the inner tension is realized.

Too frequently in Mozart, conductors get in the way of the music. With a good orchestra, often all one ought to do beyond settling certain mechanical matters about bowing is to determine the right tempo and then stand back, attending to balances as necessary and maintaining the appropriate spirit of the music. Solti's *Così fan tutte* lacks wit and sparkle because he seems to be too busy, being busy. It does not help that the production wants for a first-rate Fiordiligi.

In 1973 Solti conducted Bizet's *Carmen* at Covent Garden and recorded it two years later with the same principals. This recording is especially noteworthy for the conductor's serious attempts to come to grips with the textual disparities in the score. Any conductor of *Carmen* first must decide whether to use the *opéra-comique* version with spoken dialogue, or the more commonly-used, somewhat spurious version with accompanied recitatives. The problem is that while the recitatives are very effective, they were not composed by Bizet but added later by Ernest Guiraud. It is only in the last few years that the version with spoken dialogue has gained independent recognition. Since it is this version which Bizet apparently preferred himself, most conductors now feel that his wishes should be respected. All the recent recordings—Bernstein (DG), Abbado (DG) and Solti (Decca)—opt for the *opéra-comique* version.

The other textual issues in *Carmen* do not allow for such clear-cut solutions. They involve many minute changes in the score which have been brought to light by recent research. There are significant discrepancies between Bizet's manuscripts for the opera and the printed score (Choudens) which probably reflects what was played at the first performance in 1875. Just after 1960, the earliest manuscript copy of the score was found in a Paris library by Fritz Oeser and published by him in 1964. This new edition has forced conductors to reconsider much of the score.

Solti had been performing the traditional Choudens version for years, but when the Oeser appeared he immediately adopted it. His 1973 Covent Garden production was almost entirely the Oeser version. However, then Solti began to reconsider the relative merits of the two versions and by the time of the recording he ended up with something in between. As part of his deliberation Solti went to see Oeser and consulted also with the English scholar Winton Dean. The booklet which accompanies the Decca *Carmen* recording contains Solti's detailed notes as to why he chose one edition rather than the other at particular points in the score. It makes fascinating reading and provides a unique insight into a conductor's preparation. Here is one example concerning a passage in Act I:

In the Morales/Don José melodrama, the Oeser version includes thirty-two bars in which the dialogue is spoken over an incredibly lovely and original piece of music played by just a few instruments. It is a perfect little minor canon, precisely underlining the words. This was undoubtedly cut before the first night because it is not included in the Choudens vocal score, but I felt it may have been one of the cuts that had been forced on Bizet, and so I decided to keep the passage and follow the Oeser score. (London set OSA 13115, 1975, booklet)

The notes contain eighteen other comments of similar penetration and reasonableness. Solti concludes with a warning that not too much should be made of the disputed material, as only about ten percent of the entire score is open to this kind of debate, the remainder being identical in both versions. Solti's conducting on this recording, although less fiery than it would have been even a decade before, is tightly controlled and often quite beautiful. The cast is superb with Tatiana Troyanos, a very musical and compelling Carmen; Placido Domingo, a more interesting figure than usual for Don José; and José van Dam, a tremendously heroic Escamillo. When Abbado's version of the opera appeared in 1978, Alan Blyth of *Gramophone* compared it to Solti's and regretted the latter's lack of restraint:

Much as one admired the intelligence, musicality and care of the rival Decca performance under Solti, DG and Abbado have surpassed it by dint of adding the sense of a real and dramatic interpretation...If I could take just one moment to demonstrate the difference between Solti and Abbado it would be the orchestral phrase after José's *"Tu ne m'aimes donc plus?"* in the *Finale*. This is well enough delineated by Solti and the LPO, but Abbado, with a perfect control of the *cresc-ff-dim* asked for by Bizet and with the surge of the string playing of the LSO, ideally characterizes the desperate misery of José's feelings. Indeed, throughout this crucial scene, Abbado time and again gives that extra dimension of intensity, élan and concentration so essential to its proper execution. (October 1978)

The Solti collection of complete opera recordings continues to grow with at least a couple of new titles each year. Before long, the Wagner and Strauss canons will be virtually complete and will doubtless become one of Solti's finest achievements as a conductor. There will certainly be more

Mozart too, although one hopes to see some re-thinking on Solti's part. Further, more Verdi would be welcomed, especially an *Il Trovatore* in Vienna. With the right cast, it could be sensational.

The saddest missed opportunity, however, and there may never be another, is surely a recording of *Moses und Aron*. No one has put more effort into preparing the work and no one has conducted it more often. Solti has given three major series of performances of it at Covent Garden, the Paris Opera and with the Chicago Symphony. Why was it not recorded on one of those occasions?

8
The Interpreter on the Concert Platform

Solti is best-known today as the conductor of the Chicago Symphony, and with the recent renewal of his contract through 1982 he has decided to maintain the association. When he left Covent Garden in 1971 he made it clear that he wanted to reduce the amount of time he spent each year in the opera house. As the new conductor of one of world's best orchestras, it was assumed that his life would revolve around Chicago. But Solti is a restless and ambitious man. He not only accepted a post with the Paris Opera shortly after leaving the Royal Opera House; in addition, and at almost the same time, he took on the musical direction of the Orchestre de Paris, while continuing his involvement in Chicago. At the Paris Opera Solti contributed to an almost miraculous rejuvenation of the house, but with the orchestra, as we've already seen, the story was quite the opposite.

The Orchestre de Paris has had a short and troubled history. France has always boasted numerous orchestras, and in Paris alone there have been, at various times, at least four or five in competition with each other. Yet not one has ever become a world-class ensemble. To correct this situation, the French government created the Orchestre de Paris and brought back Charles Münch from the United States to be its conductor. Just when it seemed that the project might be on the right track, Münch died during a tour with the orchestra. So that the momentum would not be lost, the government appointed one of the best conductors of the day—Herbert von Karajan. Under Karajan, the orchestra soon reached even higher levels of achievement. But the Conductor-for-Life of the Berlin

Philharmonic was not available for more than about six weeks each year, and this simply was not enough time to produce any lasting changes. Karajan bowed out and was replaced by Solti. Again, the idea was quick improvement through the hiring of a top name.

Unfortunately, Solti's time with the orchestra was also limited. In addition, other difficulties, which Solti did not hesitate to discuss publicly, soon cropped up. Solti complained that the French musician is out for himself and dislikes working with other players as an ensemble; that he "is endowed with an natural quality of insubordination at the highest degree." (Interview in *Harmonie,* September 1974) There were reports that Solti often lost his temper in rehearsals with the orchestra because of the members' attitude. He finally gave up, deciding that he might better spend his time on other projects. Someone else could teach the orchestra how to behave:

> The professional ambition of the French orchestras is non-existent, and this is a matter of education. If an American musician makes an error during a rehearsal, nobody laughs, and one picks up immediately; in Paris that's funny and there's an uproar. (*Harmonie* interview)

Solti also claims that he was misled. He had been given to understand that Münch had held auditions to form the orchestra. In fact, fifty of the players were hired without audition. If he had known that, Solti says, he would never have accepted the position. But the orchestra had complaints of its own about the maestro which they made known after Solti's remarks to *Harmonie*. In October of 1974 *Le Monde* carried the following letter from the musicians:

> We would have liked to work with Maestro Solti more often and in a more organized manner. For that reason we deplore that he could not or thought it not necessary to be physically present at the head of the Orchestre de Paris for on the average no more than five days a month...we would have liked for Maestro Solti to show more interest in the Orchestre de Paris and for this reason, we too regret the misunderstandings, the aborted projects, the interrupted tours, the

records made elsewhere, the disappointed hopes and the bitter words, which we hope will not be all that remains of three years.

It had not helped that one Solti concert with the orchestra had been a fiasco and was reported as such in the press. It was a concert performance of Strauss' opera *Salome* with Grace Bumbry in the title role. From the beginning it was obvious that either Bumbry could not cope with the role or she was indisposed. When it came to the *Dance of the Seven Veils,* a purely orchestral section, she left the stage. In view of the taxing sections she would soon have to face it would not have been unusual for her to slip out to refresh herself. However, she simply did not reappear, leaving Solti and the Orchestre de Paris with no alternative but to grind to a halt. Solti was furious, the audience was outraged and the press tended to blame the conductor for miscasting Bumbry.

Solti had taken on the Orchestre de Paris for the same reason he had accepted a post with the Paris Opera: he believed he could help create the conditions necessary for first-class music-making. As it happened, Solti and the orchestra got off to a good start with a highly successful tour of Germany and a well-received recording of Liszt tone poems. An American tour was announced but had to be cancelled when Solti resigned. Obviously Solti has been spoiled by working with orchestras of the calibre of the Chicago Symphony, and he no longer has the patience to bring along a lesser ensemble. Even with a Solti or a Karajan on the podium it takes time to affect lasting improvements in an orchestra, and time is what such superstar conductors simply do not possess. Daniel Barenboim has succeeded Solti and has already made more recordings with the Paris Orchestra than did Karajan and Solti together. Barenboim is also a busy man, but at least he is not heading any other orchestra or opera house.

After his troubles with the Orchestre de Paris one might have expected Solti to content himself with the Chicago Symphony. What better orchestra could he head? However,

Solti's ambition is too large to keep in check. When Pierre Boulez resigned as Music Director of the New York Philharmonic Solti was under very serious consideration. Carlos Moseley, the orchestra's President, flew secretly to Europe in the spring of 1975 to offer Solti the job. Solti was tempted but finally turned it down:

> Don't think it was an easy decision; it wasn't. I love New York and the New York public. So the temptation was a big one — even with all the problems. And I knew them because I had heard the orchestra recently. (New York *Times*, May 9, 1976)

A more recent example of Solti's openness to a good offer is his acceptance of the post of Principal Conductor of the London Philharmonic. As he spends three or four months each year in England anyway, the position does not require any major disruption of his life. He will simply lend his name to the orchestra. He has already been conducting the LPO on a regular basis for many years now, and records almost as much with them as he does with the Chicago Symphony.

Solti came to regular concert conducting relatively late in his career. In fact, it was not until he took control of the Chicago Symphony in 1968 that he began to work with his own orchestra week in and week out. But since that time he has distinguished himself in quite a wide repertoire, and recordings are beginning to catch up with the amount of time he devotes to concerts. For many years his discography was dominated by operatic repertoire, with only a scattering of symphonic works. Now he is represented by all of Beethoven's major orchestral works plus the piano concertos and *Missa Solemnis*, all the Mahler symphonies, all the Schumann symphonies, and complete Brahms and Richard Strauss cycles are in progress.

The following discussion of Solti's concert conducting is organized into chronological periods of music history. Since the Beethoven and Mahler series have been dealt with at length earlier, they are not included in this chapter.

Music Before 1800

Few of the most successful conductors have shown much affinity for music before Mozart and Haydn—a not unextraordinary situation considering the fact that the symphony orchestra scarcely existed before the time of these composers. Moreover, the performances of earlier music requires both unusual orchestral (and choral) forces and often a great deal of expert research on the part of the conductor. Karajan, Stokowski and a few others have presented Monteverdi operas from time to time, but they might better leave such repertoire to the experts. While music of Bach and Handel poses fewer problems, fundamental ones still exist, particularly as far as the use of original instruments is concerned. Authentic performances of this music are becoming more common and accomplished all the time. Yet it can be argued that there will always be a place for performances of this repertoire which employ more modern forces. There is even a case to be made for traditional large-scale oratorio performances with enormous choirs and orchestras in works like *Messiah*, because so many of the essential qualities of the music survive intact. On the other hand, works such as the *Brandenburg* Concertos take on a different character altogether if too many instruments or voices are involved. A further question to be considered is whether it is appropriate to present small-scale works in enormous modern concert halls.

There appears to be just one Handel composition in Solti's active repertoire (*Concerto Grosso* Op. 3/2). Bach is only slightly better represented. In Chicago Solti has conducted some of the orchestral suites, but it is to the *St. Matthew Passion* that he returns most often. His conducting of a 1971 performance of the work was thought to be "relaxed, reverent, completely controlled," by Robert C.

Marsh of the Chicago *Sun Times* (April 1974).

Surprisingly, in view of his later career, the most prominent names in the list of composers whose pieces Solti first recorded are Mozart and Haydn: three Haydn symphonies and two by Mozart stand out in a small group which also includes Beethoven, Mendelssohn and Tchaikovsky symphonies, as well as overtures and short pieces by other composers. Solti had a reputation in his early days for enormous fire and energy in his performances, often to an excessive degree. The excitement he could whip up is amply demonstrated on the album of Suppé overtures from this period. It is an unexpected pleasure, therefore, to find that his Mozart and Haydn recordings, while exciting, are also beautifully proportioned performances.

The *Little G minor* Symphony, by its very nature, encourages a certain amount of *Sturm und Drang* from a conductor, and one might expect Solti to go overboard. He does not. And even though the constant first-beat accents in the first movement are tiresome, the playing is so well-disciplined there is no major cause for complaint. The slow movement is rather quick but Solti finds time to be expressive. The *Menuetto* is razor-sharp rhythmically and contrasts are well-judged, and the fast tempo taken in the *Finale* is under strict control. The *Prague* Symphony is also given an excellent reading—Solti avoids exaggerations and injects the performance with a great deal of life and feeling. These Mozart recordings are so good, it is a wonder that Solti has not done more; that Decca has not had him record a series of Mozart symphonies with the Vienna Philharmonic. Although Solti has been less successful with Mozart's operas, it could be that, under the right conditions, his Mozart might be as fine as anyone's.

The early Haydn recordings also reveal a fine sense of classical style. Solti was still very much under the influence of Toscanini at the time they were made, but he makes no attempt to emulate Toscanini's absurdly fast tempos. And again, there is neither exaggeration nor eccentricity.

In recent years Solti has continued to programme Mozart and Haydn at his concerts, with a heavy emphasis on the late Mozart symphonies. Evidence of a Solti performance of a Haydn symphony earlier than the set of twelve *Salomon Symphonies* does not seem to exist.

The Early Romantic Period

Among Solti's earliest recordings is a performance of Mendelssohn's *Scotch* Symphony. It is not one of the conductor's most distinguished efforts. The slower sections, the opening bars and the quiet episode just before the last movement *Coda,* for example, lack poetry, and the final *allegro maestoso* seems to be too fast for the orchestra—the sixteenth notes in the trumpets are a mess. Occasionally Solti performs other symphonies by Mendelssohn, and some by Schubert, but of the composers from the first half of the nineteenth century, with the exception of Beethoven, he has given the most attention to Schumann.

One of the major items in Solti's discography, a complete set of the Schumann symphonies with the Vienna Philharmonic, is also one of his least successful projects. In these performances he appears to equate speed with excitement. Unfortunately, what works in Suppé is disastrous in Schumann. Solti's conducting of the Second Symphony is typical of his approach to the entire set. His enthusiasm, his forward motion, his commitment, and the playing of the Vienna Philharmonic, particularly the strings, are all deserving of admiration. Yet the driving tempos taken in every movement are often clearly at variance not only with Schumann's markings in the score, but also with the style and spirit of the music.

After the slow introduction to the first movement there is a section marked *allegro ma non troppo.* If the *non troppo* is ignored, as is the case in Solti's reading, the tempo is too fast to allow for the kind of phrasing necessary to bring out the distinctive character of each musical idea. Solti sees the movement as dangerously episodic, which it is, and tries to overcome this deficiency with his hurried tempo. For all its faults, however, the music cannot stand to be rushed; it must say what it has to say in its own time. Otherwise, the numerous *crescendos* and *diminuendos* Schumann has asked for become incomprehensible. The playing at bar 210 suggest more strongly than do the tempos that conductor and orchestra alike were in too much of a hurry when they made this recording: the timpani comes in one bar early! At the climax of the movement there is a wonderfully grand peroration in the brass which the Vienna Philharmonic, under Solti, causes to sound blaring rather than noble. And why on earth is the very last chord so much louder than anything that has gone before?

The second movement *Scherzo* suffers from the same drawbacks. It is too fast, too unyielding and too messy. This movement is notoriously difficult for the violins, and even the Vienna Philharmonic players have problems at Solti's tempo. The *Finale* is again hard-driven, to the point where the orchestra has trouble maintaining ensemble and the listener has difficulty making sense of the music.

The Later Romantic Period

The favourite stamping ground of every star conductor is the music of the last half of the nineteenth century. The compositions of Brahms, Tchaikovsky, Wagner, Bruckner and Richard Strauss allow him to make use of the full modern symphony orchestra, and the style of the music encourages more freedom of expression in interpretation. Solti is not typical, therefore, in having recorded so little Brahms. A rather uninteresting recording of the Fourth Symphony has just recently appeared and the only other item in the catalogue is an ancient and pedestrian performance of the *German Requiem*, although new recordings of all the symphonies and the *Requiem* with the Chicago Symphony are expected soon.

There is more recorded evidence of Solti's thoughts on Tchaikovsky. A high voltage reading of the *Little Russian* Symphony from 1956 with the Paris Conservatory Orchestra reveals the same super-tense Solti who is so apt to go off the rails in a Schumann symphony. But, in Tchaikovsky, Solti's approach is enormously exhilarating. He attacks this repetitious, often uninspired symphony with conviction. Listeners who might be put off in the opening bars by the extreme *vibrato* in the french horn solo should bear in mind that such playing is quite conventional in France and the Soviet Union and may, in fact, be a tradition extending back to Tchaikovsky's own time. With the beginning of the *allegro vivo* Solti really comes into his own. The sound may be a little harsh and the orchestra may not be the world's finest; still, Solti gives a compelling performance. In comparison, all other recordings of this work sound mushy and dull.

Today Solti no longer attacks Tchaikovsky with the same vehemence. His 1975 recording of the Fifth Symphony is intense but heavy-handed and somehow muscle-bound. The combined energies of Solti and the Chicago Symphony cannot seem to break loose, so that the music is constricted and held back where it should be exuberant and free. I have noticed these same problems also in Solti's live performances of the Sixth: great playing from the Chicago Symphony but so tense it fails to be moving.

Because Solti has demonstrated such an extraordinary affinity for the music of Wagner, one might expect him to be equally at home in Bruckner. In fact, he is not.

He made his first recording of a Bruckner symphony (the Seventh) with the Vienna Philharmonic, as a by-product of his work on the *Ring* cycle. John Culshaw was the producer, and he brought to the recording the same spectacular sound of the *Ring* productions. It is certainly the most vivid Seventh available—every instrument comes through with wonderful presence and clarity, especially the brass—yet, this is not necessarily the ideal sound for Bruckner. DG's recording with Jochum and EMI's with Karajan both favour a quite different sound that is less immediate and more suggestive of the resonance and distance of a great cathedral. Bruckner's music has always been closely associated with the church, and while his symphonies were not necessarily conceived for church performance, the music seems to benefit from such spaciousness.

Another important difference between the Solti and the Jochum performances concerns Solti's higher degree of aggressiveness. In his recording of the Seventh, as well as the Eighth with the same orchestra, Solti encourages the brass at every opportunity; he makes more of every *crescendo;* in other words, he will not let any phrase pass without imbuing it with animation. In this way he upholds the tension and energy of the music, but he often does so at the expense of sections that depend for their effect on relaxation. And he also seriously jeopardizes the continuity of Bruckner's unusually long lines. The most difficult problem in any Bruckner symphony is maintaining the flow—bridging the silent bars, rests, string temolos, soft timpani rolls, etc., between different themes and episodes. The tension cannot be allowed to sag in such passages. Jochum, who is recognized as one of the greatest living interpreters of Bruckner, realizes that the supposed gaps in the music must be played with as much care as the notes, and thus he demonstrates a better understanding of the shape of Bruckner's long phrases and large movements than does Solti. Jochum has been criticized for sometimes altering Bruckner's tempo instructions, but the criticism is not a serious one. Certain tempo adjustments are necessary and many of Jochum's are quite inspired.

Karajan, and especially Furtwängler, are also highly regarded as Bruckner conductors, and not least of all because of a similar ability to maintain tension over long periods. Karajan, however, tends to be rather rigid in sticking to one basic tempo for each movement, and although this is admirable in principle it occasionally leads to monotony. In comparison to the competition, and in light of his Wagner accomplishments, Solti's recorded Bruckner has been disappointing. Nevertheless, he is intent on doing more: a complete cycle of all the symphonies is a distinct possibility. It might well be that the older Solti will take a larger view of these works than did the younger.

Just as Solti's Wagner does not prepare one for his Bruckner, his conducting of Strauss' tone poems does not measure up to his fine handling of *Electra* and *Salome*.

Don Juan begins with Solti's customary energy, and here energy is just what is needed. But Solti renders the love music square and uninflected, and at the end there is not much of a climax. The final bars are too loud to be poignant. It all passes with a quickness that hinders listener involvement. "After all," Solti seems to be saying, "this is only a showpiece for a virtuoso orchestra." There is more character in *Till Eulenspiegel*, even though the heavy accentuation becomes quite tiresome in spite of the brilliant playing.

Zarathustra is given an exciting reading that is wonderfully exact rhythmically, and which drives forward impressively. For all Solti's concern with rhythm and clarity, however, he does not bring out the dotted timpani figure at the climax as successfully as Karajan does in his DG recording. And while Karajan's tempo is much slower, he not only manages to be just as spirited as Solti, he also finds more substance in nearly every section of the score. The eloquence of the B major final section in his performance is not even hinted at in Solti's. The Chicago strings lack colour and sensitivity, and the bass and cello *pizzicato* notes in the last bars are far too loud. Perhaps the worst failing of the Solti recording is the violin solo. Technically the playing is well below what one would expect from a concertmaster of the Chicago Symphony, and musically it is a non-starter alongside Schwalbé for Karajan.

Among the most intriguing and unexpected additions to Solti's repertoire in recent years are the orchestral works of Sir Edward Elgar. Few conductors of European origin have paid the slightest attention to the English composer's music, and audiences in Budapest, Vienna and Hamburg do not seem anxious to change this situation. Solti's interest in Elgar is, therefore, somewhat anomalistic, although it is not surprising. During his long period in charge of Covent Garden, Solti developed a great fondness for England which continues to this day, and which inevitably came to include some of the country's music. He conducted Britten at Covent Garden and more recently has given performances of major works by Walton and Tippett. With his liking for Strauss, it is natural that Solti should be attracted to those qualities in Elgar common to both composers.

British music critics have tended to be patronizing about performances of English music by non-English conductors, and not always without justification. A Boult or a Barbirolli does seem to bring to his reading a special quality which eludes a Toscanini, a Karajan or a Bernstein. But while Solti's Elgar has it deficiencies, they are not really due to his lacking a special "Englishness." In his recording of the First Symphony, for example, towards the end of the first movement where Barbirolli captures a wonderful wistfulness, Solti merely plays the notes. Similarly, in the beginning of the last movement, Barbirolli achieves a poetic tenderness which has characteristically eluded Solti, not only in Elgar's music but in the works of other composers as well.

Solti has said that he listened to Elgar's recordings in preparing his own, and generally speaking the broad outlines of both are the same. What Solti often misses is much of the detail. For instance, again in the First Symphony, Elgar has not called for a slowing up in the score just before 108 in the last movement introduction, yet he himself reduces speed markedly on the last two notes, and he does so again before 110. Solti chooses not to, thereby forfeiting a very pleasing effect. It is touches of this sort which individualize a performance and give the music more character even, it would appear, if that music is one's own. Further, Solti's loud and intense *grandioso* final section lacks breadth. And before 148, where Elgar has carefully worked out the dynamics so that the right voices emerge at the right time — a scheme which works to perfection in his own recording, with trumpets and trombones giving way to the horns, and then reasserting themselves — Solti has decided to virtually ignore the composer's instructions.

On the other hand, there is a great deal to enjoy in Solti's rendition of the First. Most memorable of all, perhaps, is the way he tears into the *allegro* of the last movement. Also, the standard of playing is exceptionally high.

Solti's recording of the *Enigma* Variations is undoubtedly one of the best the work has ever had. The London Philharmonic does well with the symphonies for Solti, but the Chicago Symphony is better still. The trumpets are always dead-on in rhythm and intonation, the clarity of the timpani in the lightning-fast variation 7 is incredible, and the solo cello in variation 12 is the work of a great artist. From the opening bars Solti conveys a feeling of deep involvement with the music, and the impression is maintained throughout. I would prefer to hear more of the organ in the *Finale* and more G-string tone from the violins; however the engineers may be at fault here.

Music of the Twentieth Century

As was noted in an earlier chapter, Solti has programmed more contemporary music than some of his critics are prepared to admit. To date, though, his interest does not extend to recording. Naturally, there is a limited market for new music, but Solti's name on the record jacket would increase that market considerably. Star conductors have a special obligation to employ their talents and the power of their reputation in the service of living composers. There is no question that the repertoire is revitalized thereby. Serge Koussevitsky almost single-handedly created a new literature of important orchestral works by American composers, and his example has been followed by his prize student, Leonard Bernstein.

By far the most frequently-programmed twentieth century music in Solti's repertoire is that of fellow-Hungarian and former teacher, Béla Bartók. Solti has presented all-Bartók concerts from time to time and is justly famous for his performances. Among his early batch of recordings are two Bartók works, both of them since re-recorded, and others have followed. Solti conducts Bartók well, not simply because he knew the composer nor because they shared a common nationality, but because of the rhythmic intricacies of these works which Solti is able to clarify so skilfully. His Bartók recordings can stand today as being the standard versions, although they would have been even better had they been done in Chicago: the trumpet playing from the London Symphony in the *Concerto for Orchestra* is well below what one might reasonably expect.

Due to Solti's success with Schönberg's opera *Moses und Aron*, more performances of both Schönberg's music and the music of other composers of the New Vienna School would seem to be in order. In fact, this one opera aside, Solti has paid scant attention to the works of either Schönberg, Berg or Webern. His only recording of a piece by any of these composers is Schönberg's *Variations* Op. 31 with the Chicago Symphony, an extremely difficult work for performers and listeners alike. Unfortunately, while there are passages of remarkable virtuosity in Solti's recording, the players are not at their best. Perhaps there was insufficient rehearsal time. Also, Solti does not really penetrate beneath the surface of the music. The theme is hauntingly expressive in its first statement in the cellos, and is no less so near the end in the solo violin, but each time Solti and his men are content simply to play the notes. Compare Karajan with the Berlin Philharmonic. He finds a whole range of dynamic inflections and tonal colours not even suggested in the Solti recording. Even though the trumpets of the Berlin Philharmonic do not play with the security of the Chicago musicians, one gains a far greater sense of the character of each variation and of the logic of the whole from the Karajan recording.

Solti has conducted a fair number of Stravinsky's works over the years although, like Karajan, he has not concerned himself with either *Petrouchka* or the *Firebird*. Again, as in the case of Bartók, his rhythmic control is an important asset. In a score such as *Le Sacre du Printemps,* Solti's nervous energy is a further advantage. With the Chicago Symphony to play the notes and the Decca engineers to record them, all the elements existed to make Solti's recording of this ballet music first-class. Some of the subtle colouration is missing; still, one can scarcely complain when so much else has been captured.

With some exceptions noted earlier, Solti's recorded repertoire has come more and more to reflect his range as a conductor. By temperament and experience he would seem to be especially well-equipped to deal with late romantic and early twentieth century repertoire. Yet, much of his recorded output in these areas has been below expectations. However, Solti is continuing to grow as a conductor and interpreter, and substantial improvement in his weaker areas is certainly a possibility.

9
A Summing Up

I firmly believe that the essential quality of a conductor is, first of all, that power to project your imagination to other people. (Solti, in conversation with Norman Pelligrini for the WFMT programme *Profiles of Greatness,* November 28, 1974)

Whatever criticisms one might have about Solti's handling of particular pieces, it can scarcely be denied that he possesses all the attributes of a fine conductor. His preparation for the podium was solid in the old-fashioned European way: he became highly proficient at the keyboard; he coached in an opera house; and he was exposed to, and thereby learned from, some outstanding conductors during his formative years. Furthermore, he has an excellent ear, a reliable if unorthodox baton technique, and is equally at home in virtually any part of the standard orchestral and operatic literature. But, as he himself has pointed out, his most valuable asset is his ability to project his imagination to others.

As a physical presence, Solti is a compelling man. He exudes energy and authority through his bearing: jaw set, eyes blazing, body coiled and restless. His enormous communicative powers are evident in all his performances, whether he takes charge of a concert, an opera or a recording session. But while the fact of this ability is undeniable, there is by no means general agreement concerning its quality. Over the years Solti has had prominent and persistent detractors. One of them is the conductor and writer Robert Lawrence, who dislikes even the most widely admired Solti recordings:

The negative reaction stems largely from his recordings of the *Ring, Salome, Electra,* with their abdication of the right to mold sonorities of his [sic] own, balance instruments and voices perceptively, work for organic tone. Studio forces have taken over instead with crude, blow-up insistence. Nor have I been overwhelmed in the flesh by an adroit but undistinguished *Tannhäuser, Don Carlos.* (*A Rage for Opera,* 1971)

The New York *Times'* Senior Music Critic, Harold C. Schonberg, has echoed this view more recently with reference to Solti's recordings of the Beethoven symphonies:

Even Mr. Solti's set, for all the instrumental glamour and occasional punchy excitement, seems to lack a distinctive overall point of view. (New York *Times,* May 7, 1978)

If Lawrence and Schonberg have found Solti often superficial and uninteresting, other critics have taken issue with his aggressiveness. Adrian Jack, covering a performance of the Mahler Sixth with the London Philharmonic, had this to report:

In the first movement he invariably gave predominance to brass themes, even though some of them are secondary: too often the horns let rip so that the woodwind and strings were smothered. The whole of the first subject-group was played as if by a brass band composed of thugs. (*Music and Musicians,* July 1974)

Harold Schonberg has also complained about this aspect of Solti's conducting. Reviewing a Carnegie Hall performance of *The Flying Dutchman* he registered a strong complaint about the decibel level:

Can Georg have forgotten that the difference between heavy volume and sheer noise can sometimes be a hairline distinction? He conducted the orchestra with such enthusiasm that the results occasionally approached aural pain. He has one of the most powerful orchestras in the business — those brasses! — and is himself an ardent, impetuous musician. All that, together with Carnegie Hall sound, made for some very noisy happenings during the evening. (New York *Times,* May 16, 1976)

The Editor of the *Musical Newsletter* was even more vehement in his remarks about the same concert:

> Solti had mercilessly stomped on a work that deserved far different handling, and had produced a crude and vulgar slam-bang rather than a musical performance. (Vol. VI, No. 2, Spring 1976)

Nicholas Kenyon had a similar reaction to most performances given by Solti with the London Philharmonic in an extended series of concerts at the Festival Hall in February and March of 1977. Kenyon was particularly impatient with a reading of Walton's *Belshazzar's Feast:*

> Once again going for the dramatic effect and once again ignoring moments of lyricism and bulldozing his way through the score, he seemed concerned only to generate thrills, and instead produced a brash and nasty rush across the surface of the music which was anything but thrilling. (*Music and Musicians,* May 1977, p. 47)

Such comments have dogged Solti almost from the earliest stages of his career. On the other hand, in all the same places where Solti has been dealt with harshly, he has also been extravagantly praised by other critics, and audiences have often cheered him for as much as half an hour after a performance.

When Solti conducted Brahms' *A German Requiem* in New York recently—and this is a work which demands the utmost sensitivity and taste to perform—Raymond Ericson declared that it was the best performance of the work he had ever heard:

> Mr. Solti, with a superb orchestra and chorus at his command, seemed to do everything exactly right. What many consider to be flaws in his performances, the slick, high-powered drive, the theatricalization of detail, were absent. Yet there was enough sense of calculation left to keep the music poised and flowing. The tempos were perfectly set to establish the indicated mood and then never allowed to sag. The few liberties that were taken, broad *ritards* at the end of a couple of movements, were logical. (New York *Times,* May 14, 1978)

Discussing a 1971 concert performance of *Das Rheingold* by Solti and the Chicago Symphony, Roger Dettmer likewise reached for the most extreme compliments:

> The stars were Solti—in an unusually expansive mood—and the orchestra played for him with a splendour unequaled in my experience of any *Ring* opera, on whatever continent, whether live or recorded, in an opera house or on a concert stage. (*Opera,* December 1971)

Even Harold Schonberg has frequently been lavish in his praise of Solti. He is on record as preferring Solti's *Ring* cycle—"monumental in conception" (New York *Times,* November 28, 1976) to Karajan's, and in 1963 he was most enthusiastic about a performance of *Aïda* at the Metropolitan Opera:

> There were some remarkably fine things in the musical end. Chief among these...Georg Solti. His conducting was all fire, lyricism and imagination...By touching up a tempo here, by inserting a few *ritards* and *fermatas,* by adjusting the balances so that Verdi's orchestration could come through, by not being afraid to let loose when necessary, Mr. Solti provided almost a new light on the opera. (New York *Times,* October 15, 1963)

Alan Rich of *New York* magazine has summed up most succinctly the sentiment of so many of Solti's admirers in calling him "a shoo-in for World's Best Conductor title." (September 20, 1976)

Solti is certainly one of our finest musicians, however surprisingly enough, few of his recordings are truly memorable. As certain of his critics have been quick to point out, he is not without his problems, and among the most serious are extreme aggressiveness and lack of depth.

Harold Schonberg has written that "Solti never makes a rhythmic mistake," (New York *Times,* November 28, 1976) and while, literally, Schonberg is quite correct, such approbation is misleading. Solti is almost pathologically concerned that rhythmic patterns be played correctly and that the metric pulse of every score be realized. But the result is often overemphasis on rhythmic accentuation which, in turns, leads to an unpleasant heaviness. Even where no accent is written—at the beginning of a bar or on strong beats in general—Solti usually supplies one. He does this so often it has become a mannerism, even a trademark. Ironically, the conductor most concerned with rhythmic accuracy is the conductor who so frequently distorts it.

Solti's general lack of expansiveness in his phrasing—his unwillingness to produce a singing line, particularly in loud and heavily-scored passages—is another of his shortcomings. There is a tightness, unpleasantly military in its feeling, which robs much of the music he conducts of its nobility. Also to be lamented is his inability to unify scores organically. He has the energy and the concentration, but seldom the willingness to make all the details relate to a conception of the whole. I often come away from a Solti performance feeling that I heard every note of the piece played yet somehow missed hearing the work as a whole.

However, Solti is still very much in the prime of his career, and there are signs that he is continuing to grow. He came to Mahler quite late and already has achieved remarkable results with his music. Elgar, too, is a composer to whom Solti was not introduced until recently, and he can be expected to do greater justice to Elgar's works in the years to come. Solti himself speaks of exploring new repertoire, including Sibelius symphonies which he has never conducted before.

And if Solti seems to fall short as an interpreter, certain of his achievements are far from disappointing. A long list of musical institutions are healthier today because he was in charge of them. The Royal Opera House, Covent Garden, the Paris Opera and, above all, the Chicago Symphony are deeply in his debt. His success with any one of these organizations would be enough to warrant his eminent reputation.

Discography

This discography is comprehensive as of February 1979 and includes all Solti's commercial recordings known to us. It does not include projected releases which are tentative.

The following orchestras and choirs are abbreviated in these listings as indicated. Instrumentalists and singers, whose surnames only are used within the discography, are indentified below.

CHOIRS

ASCC	Accademia di Santa Cecilia, Rome
CSC	Chicago Symphony
CCC	Chichester Cathedral
FOMC	Frankfurt Opera and Museum
GSC	Gumpoldskirchner Spatzen
CHS	Haperdasher's School, Elstree
JAC	John Alldis
LSOC	London Symphony Orchestra
RCAC	RCA Italian Opera
ROC	Rome Opera
ROHC	Royal Opera House Covent Garden
SCC	Salisbury Cathedral
VBC	Vienna Boys
VGM	Vienna Gesellschaft
VSC	Vienna Singverein
VSOC	Vienna State Opera
WCC	Winchester Cathedral

ORCHESTRAS

ASCO	Accademia di Santa Cecilia, Rome
BSOO	Bavarian State Opera
BPO	Berlin Philharmonic
CLOO	Chicago Lyric Opera
CSO	Chicago Symphony
COA	Concertgebouw Orchestra of Amsterdam
FOMO	Frankfurt Opera and Museum
IPO	Israel Philharmonic
LPO	London Philharmonic
LSO	London Symphony
O de P	Orchestre de Paris
PCO	Paris Conservatory
RCAO	RCA Italian
ROO	Rome Opera
ROHO	Royal Opera House, Covent Garden
TOZ	Tonhalle Orchestra, Zurich
VPO	Vienna Philharmonic

PIANISTS
Vladimir Ashkenazy
Clifford Curzon

Alicia de Larrocha
Julius Katchen

VIOLINISTS
Kyung-Wha Chung
Mischa Elman

Georg Kulenkampf

SINGERS
Theo Adam
Ewald Aichberger
Thomas Allen
Wolfgang Appel
Libero Arbace

Gabriel Bacquier
Norman Bailey
Janet Baker
Oda Balsborg
Ettore Bastianini
Margarethe Bence
Jane Berbié
Teresa Berganza
H.H. Berger-Tuna
Carlo Bergonzi
Walter Berry
Judith Blegen
Hannelore Bode
Kurt Böhme
Hans Braun
Victor Braun
Delme Bryne-Jones
Grace Bumbry
Norma Burrowes
Stuart Burrow

Montserrat Caballé
Joan Carlyle
Plinio Clabassi
Marie Collier
Fernando Corena
Mini Cörtse
Carlos Cossutta
Régine Crespin

Adolf Dallapozza
Ryland Davies
Stafford Dean
Lisa Della Casa
Anny Delorie
Piero de Palma
Anton Dermota
Helga Dernesch
Christina Deutekom
Murray Dickie
John Dobson
Placido Domingo
Helen Donath

Nigel Douglas
Peter Dvorsky

Otto Edelmann
Martin Egel
Rosalind Elias
Kurt Equiluz
Geraint Evans

Brigitte Fassbänder
Birgit Finnila
Dietrich Fischer-Dieskau
Ezio Flagello
Kirsten Flagstad
Ferdinand Frantz
Mirella Freni
Gottlob Frick

Aron Gestner
Nicolai Ghiaurov
Christel Goltz
Rita Gorr
Edita Gruberova
Hilde Güden
Maureen Guy

Julia Hamari
Retraud Hansliann
Alison Hargan
Heather Harper
Rudolf Hartmann
Claudia Hellman
Judith Hellwig
Hans Helm
Marga Höffgen
Grace Hoffman
Heinz Holecek
Werner Hollweg
Elisabeth Höngen
Marilyn Horne
Hans Hotter
Gwynne Howell
Anne Howells

Alfred Jerger
Gwyneth Jones
Manfred Jungwirth

Zoltan Kélémen

152

David Kelly
James King
Theodore Kirschbichler
Peter Klein
Werner Klumlikboldt
Waldemar Kmentt
Gillian Knight
René Kollo
Zenon Koznowski
Ernst Kozub
Adalbert Kraus
Alfredo Kraus
Tom Krause
Werner Krenn
Walter Kreppel
Teresa Kubiak
Paul Kuen
Erich Kunz

Herbert Lachner
Michael Langdon
Max Lichtegg
Ilva Ligabue
Margarita Lilowa
Berit Lindholm
Vera Little
George London
Emmy Loose
Pilar Lorengar
Veriana Luchetti
Christa Ludwig

Cornell MacNeil
Liselotte Maikl
Ira Malaniuk
Janis Martin
William McAlpine
Alec McCowen
Kenneth McDonald
Donald McIntyre
Robert Merrill
Kerstin Meyer
Sherrill Milnes
Yvonne Minton
Anna Moffo
Kurt Moll

Gustav Neidlinger
Gerd Nienstedt
Birgit Nilsson

Luciano Pavarotti
Peter Pears
Jo Ann Pickens
Hetty Plümacher
Lucia Popp
Hermann Prey
Leontyne Price

Margaret Price
Herbert Prikopa
Max Proebstl
Harold Proglhof

Franco Racciardi
Rugg Raimondi
Regina Resnik
Forbes Robinson
Ann Robson
Frieda Rösler
Michel Roux
Kurt Rydl

Marianne Schech
Marga Schiml
Anny Schlemm
Vera Schlosser
Martin Schomberg
Rosi Schwaiger
Stepan Schwer
Michel Sénéchal
Mietta Sighele
Giulietta Simionato
Hans Sotin
Sylvia Stahlman
Ilona Steingruber
Gerhard Stolze
Joan Sutherland
Set Svanholm

Martti Talvela
Robert Tear
Renata Tebaldi
Kiri Te Kanawa
Karl Terkal
Pierre Thau
Giorgio Tozzi
Tatiana Troyanos
Marilyn Tyler

Fritz Uhl

Anita Välkki
Henneke van Bork
José van Dam
Arnold van Mill
Josephine Veasey
Jon Vickers

Eberhard Wächter
Mallory Walker
Claire Watson
Helen Watts
Bernd Weikl
Otto Wiener
Wolfgang Windgassen
Lore Wismann
Erwin Wohlfahrt

Heinz Zednik

153

KEY TO RECORD IDENTIFICATION

U.K. disc numbers appear first. Many of the recordings have been recoupled or repackaged. Only the original or most usual issues are shown. Some are available on cassette, eight-track and reel-to-reel tapes. Consult catalogues for availability.

Chicago Symphony Society:	CSO 1000
U.S. Capitol:	Mono – PRB
CETRA, Italy:	Mono – LO
D.G.:	Mono – DGM 12" 78 RPM – 68000
English Decca:	Stereo – ... BB..., D...D, ECS, GOS, JB, SDD, SET, SPA, SXL Mono – ACL, ECM, LW, LXT 12" 78 RPM – K
U.S. Decca:	Mono – DL
London:	Stereo – CS, CSA, CSP, OS, OSA, RDNS, S, STS Mono – A, CM LL, R
English RCA:	Stereo – RL, SER
U.S. RCA:	Stereo – ARL, LSC

SOLTI AS PIANIST
BEETHOVEN, Ludwig van
   Violin Sonata in A Op. 47 (Kreutzer)
   Kulenkampf

7/48	ECM 832	R 23214

BRAHMS, Johannes
   Violin Sonatas No.'s 1 in G Op. 78, 2 in A Op. 100 and 3 in D minor Op. 108
   Kulenkampf

2/47 & 7/48	ECM 831	R 23213

MOZART, Wolfgang Amadeus
   Violin Sonata in B flat K. 454
   Kulenkampf

6/47	ECM 832	R 23214

SCHUBERT, Franz
   Schwanengesang: No. 7 Abschied, No. 6 In der Ferne
   Lichtegg

c. 1945	K 2172

SOLTI AS PERCUSSIONIST *
MOZART, Wolfgang Amadeus
   Magic Flute K. 620 (conductor – Toscanini)

1937 Salzburg	LO 44

* Solti's first exposure on record, playing the glockenspiel

154

BARTÓK, Béla

Concerto for Orchestra

LSO	2/65	SXL 6212	CS 6784

Dance Suite

LPO	11/52	ECS 533	LL 709
LSO	2/65	SXL 6212	CS 6784

The Miraculous Mandarin – Suite Op 19

LSO	12/63	SXL 6111	CS 6783

Music for Strings, Percussion and Celesta

LPO	4/55	ECS 533	LL 709
LSO	12/63	SXL 6111	CS 6783

Violin Concerto No. 2 in B minor
Chung

LPO	2/76	SXL 6802	CS 7023

BEETHOVEN, Ludwig van

Coriolanus Overture Op. 62

CSO	9/74	11BB188/96	CSP 9

Egmont Op. 84 and Leonore No. 3 Op. 72 Overtures

TOZ	c. 1948		LL 49
CSO	5/72	11BB188/96	CSP 9

Fidelio Op. 72: Act I – Mir ist so Wunderbar
Robson, Jones, Kelly, Dobson

ROHO	3-7/68	SET 392/3	OSA 1276

Missa Solemnis Op. 123
Popp, Minton, Walker, Howell

CSC/CSO	5/77	D87D 2	OSA 12111

Piano Concertos: Complete
Ashkenazy

CSO	5/72	SXL (G) 6594/7	OSA 2404

Symphonies No. 1-9 (including conversation between Solti and music critic William Mann – English Decca only)

CSO	9/74	11BB188/96	CSP 9

Sympony No. 3 in E flat Op. 55

VPO	5/59	SXL 2165	CS 6778

Symphony No. 4 in B flat Op. 60

LPO	11/50	ECS 556	LL 319

Symphony No. 5 in C minor Op. 67

VPO	9-10/58	SXL 2124	CS 6092

Symphony No. 7 in A Op. 92

VPO	9-10/58	SXL 2121	CS 6777

Symphony No. 9 in D minor Op. 125
Lorengar, Minton, Burrows, Talvela

CSC/CSO	5/72		CSP 8

Symphony No. 9 excerpts from London recording. "The Making of a Masterwork..." Solti comments with chorus master Margaret Hillis. Produced as a membership bonus for members of the Chicago Symphony Society.

CSC/CSO	1973		CSO 1000

Violin Concerto in D Op. 61
LPO

Elman	4/55	LXT 5068	LL 1257

BERLIOZ, Hector
Les Francs-Juges — Overture Op. 3

CSO	5/72	SXL 6684	

Symphonie Fantastique Op. 14

CSO	5/72	SXL 6571	CS 6790

BIZET, Georges
Carmen: Prelude to Act I

ROHO	3/68	SET 392/3	OSA 1276

: Complete
Troyanos, Domingo, Te Kanawa, van Dam, Burrowes, Berbié, Roux, Senechal, Allen, Thua

CHS/JAC/LPO	7/75	D11D 3	OSA 13115

BOÏTO, Arrigo
Mefistofele: L'altre notte
Tebaldi

CLOO	c. 1956	LXT 5326	A 5320

BORODIN, Alexander
Prince Igor: Overture

BPO	6/59	SPA 257	CS 6944
LSOC/LSO	12/65	SXL 6684	CS 6800

: Polovtsian Dances

LSOC/LSO	5/66	SXL 6263	CS 6785

BRAHMS, Johannes
German Requiem Op. 45
Adam, Wismann

FOMC/FOMO	c. 1954		PRB 8300

Symphony No. 4 in E minor Op. 98

CSO	5/78	SXL 6890	

BRITTEN, Benjamin
Billy Budd: Act I — O Beauty, O Handsomeness, Goodness
Robinson

ROHO	3-7/68	SET 392/3	OSA 1276

A Midsummer Night's Dream: Act 3 — Helena!...Hermia
Bryn-Jones, McDonald, Robson, Howells

ROHO	3-7/68	SET 392/3	OSA 1276

BRUCKNER, Anton
Symphony No. 7 in E

VPO	11/65	SET 323/4	CSA 2216

Symphony No. 8 in C minor

VPO	11-12/66	SET 335/6	CSA 2219

DEBUSSY, Claude
La Mer
CSO	5/76	SXL 6813	CS 7033

Prélude à l'Après-midi d'un faune
CSO	5/76	SXL 6813	CS 7033

DUKAS, Paul
The Sorcerer's Apprentice
IPO	4/57	ECS 703	STS 15005

ELGAR, Edward
Cockaigne Overture Op. 40
LPO	2/76	SXL 6795	CS 7072

Enigma Variations Op. 36
CSO	5/74	SXL 6795	CS 6984

God Save the King (arr. Elgar)
LPO	2-3/77	SXL 6848	CS 7072

Pomp and Circumstance Marches 1-5 Op. 39
LPO	2-3/77	SXL 6848	CS 7072

Symphony No. 1 in A flat Op. 55
LPO	2/72	SXL 6569	CS 6789

Symphony No. 2 in E flat Op. 63
LPO	2/75	SXL 6723	CS 6941

Violin Concerto in B minor Op. 61
Chung
LPO	2/77	SXL 6842	CS 7064

GIORDANO, Umberto
Andrea Chenier: Nemico della patria
Bastianini
CLOO	c. 1956	LXT 5326	A 5320

GLINKA, Michael Ivanovitch
Ruslan and Ludmilla: Overture
BPO	6/59	SPA 257	CS 6944
LSO	12/65	SXL 6263	CS 6785

GLUCK, Christoph Willibald
Orfeo ed Euridice
Horne, Lorengar, Donath
ROHC/ROHO	7/69	SET 443/4	OSA 1285

GOUNOD, Charles
Faust: Ballet Music
ROHO	5/60	JB 12	CS 6780

HAYDN, Franz Joseph
Symphony No. 100 in G
LPO	4/54	LXT 2984	CM 9106

Symphony No. 102 in B flat
LPO	11/51	LXT 2984	CM 9106

Symphony No. 103 in E flat
LPO   8/49   ACL 107   LL 557

HOLST, Gustav Theodore
The Planets Op. 32
LPO   2/78   SET 628   CS 7110

HUMPERDINCK, Engelbert
Hänsel und Gretel
Popp, Fässbander, Berry, Hamari, Schlemm, Burrows, Gruberova
VBC/VPO   2-3-6/78   D131D 2

KODÁLY, Zoltán
Dances of Galanta
LPO   11/52   ECS 519   LL 709

Háry János: Suite
BSOO   c. 1948   68392/94   DL 9518
LPO   4/55   ECS 519   CM 9132

Peacock Variations
LPO   4/54   ECS 519   LL 1020

Psalmus Hungaricus Op. 13
McAlpine
LPC/LPO   5/54   ECS 533   LL 1020

LISZT, Franz
Mephisto Waltz No. 1
O de P   6/74   SXL 6709   CS 6925

Symphonic Poems: Tasso, From the Cradle to the Grave
O de P   6/74   SXL 6709   CS 6925
        : Prometheus, Les Préludes, Festklänge
LPO   4-6/77   SXL 6863   CS 7084

MAHLER, Gustav
Das Knaben Wunderhorn No.'s 2, 5, 7 and 9
Minton
CSO   2-4/70   SET 471/2   CSA 2228

Das Lied von der Erde
Minton, Kollo
CSO   5/72   SET 555   OS 26292

Lieder eines fahrenden Gesellen
Minton
CSO   3-4/70   SET 469/70   CSA 2227

Symphony No. 1 in D
LSO   1-2/64   SXL 6113   CS 6401

Symphony No. 2 in C minor
Harper, Watts
LSOC/LSO   5/66   SET 325/6   CSA 2217

Symphony No. 3 in D minor
Watts
LSOC/LSO   1/68   SET 385/6   CSA 2223

Symphony No. 4 in G
Stahlman
COA   2/61   SXL 2276   CS 6781

Symphony No. 5 in C sharp minor
CSO   3-4/70   SET 471/2   CSA 2228
Symphony No. 6 in A minor
CSO   3-4/70   SET 469/70   CSA 2231

Symphony No. 7 in E minor
CSO   5/71   SET 518/9   CSA 2231

Symphony No. 8 in E
Harper, Popp, Kollo, Watts, Talvela
VSC/CSO   8-9/71   SET 534/5   OSA 1295

Symphony No. 9 in D
LSO   4-5/67   SET 385/6   CSA 2220

MENDELSSOHN, Felix
Symphony No. 3 in A minor Op. 56
LSO   11/52   ECS 527   LL 708

Symphony No. 4 in A Op. 90
IPO   5/58   SDD 121   STS 15008

MOZART, Wolfgang Amadeus
Così fan tutte K. 588
Lorengar, Berganza, Davies, Bacquier, Krause, Berbié
ROHC/LPO   7/73 & 2/74   SET 575/8   OSA 1442

Eine kleine Nachtmusik K. 525 (Serenade No. 13)
IPO   10/58   SXL 2046   STS 15141

Magic Flute K. 620
Lorengar, Deutekom, Burrows, Talvela, Prey, Plümacher, Sotin, Fischer-
Dieskau, Equiluz, van Bork, Minton, Stolze, Kollo, Lachner
VBC/VSOC/
VPO   9-10/69   SET 479/81   OSA 1397

Marriage of Figaro K. 492: Voi che sapete
Simionato
CLOO   c. 1956   LXT 5326   A 5320
                        : Dove Sono
Carlyle
ROHO   3-7/68   SET 392/3   OSA 1276

Piano Concertos No.'s 25 K. 503 and 27 K. 595
de Larrocha
LPO   12/77   SX 6887   CS 7109

Symphonies No. 25 in G minor K. 183 and 38 in D K. 504
LPO   4/51   ECS 591   LL 1034

MUSSORGSKY, Modest Petrovitch
Khovanschina: Prelude
BPO   6/59   SPA 257   CS 6944
LSO   12/65   SXL 6263   CS 6785
                        : Dance of the Persian Slaves
BPO   6/59   SPA 257   CS 6944

A Night on the Bare Mountain
BPO   6/59   SPA 257   CS 6944
LSO   12/65   SXL 6263   CS 6785

OFFENBACH, Jacques
Gaité Parisienne (arr. Rosenthal)
ROHO   2/61   JB 12   CS 6780

Tales of Hoffman: Barcarolle
ROHO   6/58   SPA 347   CS 6753

PONCHIELLI, Amilcare
La Gioconda: L'amo come il fulgor
Simionato, Tebaldi
CLOO   c. 1956   LXT 5326   A 5320
            : Dance of the Hours
ROHO   6/58   SPA 347   CS 6753

PUCCINI, Giacomo
La Bohème
Caballé, Domingo, Milnes, Raimondi, Blegen
JAC/LPO   1973   ARL 2-0371

RACHMANINOFF, Sergei
Piano Concerto No. 2 in C minor Op. 18
Katchen
LSO   6/58   SDD 181   STS 15086

RAVEL, Maurice
Boléro
CSO   5/76   SXL 6813   CS 7033

RESPIGHI, Ottorino
La boutique fantasque
IPO   4/57   SPA 376   STS 15005

ROSSINI, Gioacchino
Barber of Seville: Overture
LPO   4/55   LW 5207
CSO   5/72   SXL 6684   CS 6800

L'Italiana in Algeri: Overture
LPO   2/55   LW 5207
ROHO   6/58   SPA 347   CS 6753

Semiramide: Overture
ROHO   6/58   SPA 347   CS 6753

SAINT-SAENS, Camille
Samson et Dalila: Mon coeur s'ouvra à ta voix
Simionato
CLOO   c. 1956   LXT 5326   A 5320

SCHÖNBERG, Arnold
Variations for Orchestra Op. 31
CSO   5/74   CS 6984

160

SCHUBERT, Franz
  Symphony No. 5 in B flat
    IPO   5/58   SDD 121   STS 15008

SCHUMANN, Robert
  Julius Caesar: Overture
    VPO   9/69   SXL 6487   CSA 2310

  Overture, Scherzo and Finale Op. 52
    VPO   9/69   SXL 6486   ĊS 6696

  Symphony No. 1 in B flat Op. 38
    VPO   9/69   SXL 6486   CS 6696

  Symphony No. 2 in C Op. 61
    VPO   9/69   SXL 6487   CSA 2310

  Symphonies No. 3 in E flat Op. 97 and 4 in D minor Op. 120
    VPO   11/67   SXL 6356   CS 6582

STRAUSS, Richard
  Also sprach Zarathustra Op. 30
    CSO   5/75   SXL 6749   CS 6978

  Arabella
    Della Casa, London, Edelmann, Güden, Dermota, Malaniuk, Kmentt,
    Wächter, Proglhof, Cörtse, Hellwig
    VSOC/VPO   8/57   GOS 571/3   S 63522

  Ariadne auf Naxos
    Price, Troyanos, Kollo, Kunz, Gruberova, Berry
    LPO   11-12/77   D103D 3

  Don Juan Op. 20
    CSO   5/72   SXL 6749   CS 6978

  Elektra: Ich will Nichts horen, Was willst du, fremder Mensch
    Höngen, Goltz, Frantz
    BSOO   c. 1949   DGM 19038   DL 9723
      : Complete
    Nilsson, Resnik, Krause, Collier, Stolze
    VSOC/VPO   9/66 & 9/67   SET 354/5   OSA 1269

  Ein Heldenleben Op. 40
    VPO   3/77   SET 601   CS 7083

  Der Rosenkavalier
    Crespin, Minton, Jungwirth, Wiener, Donath, Loose, Dickie, Howells,
    Lachner, Prikopa, Equiluz, Jerger, Dermota, Pavarotti, Schwaiger, Terkal
    VSOC/VPO   11/68   SET 418/21   OSA 1435
      : Act 2 – Da lieg'ich, Herr Kavalier
    Langdon, Minton
    ROHO   3-7/78   SET 392/3   OSA 1276

  Salome
    Nilsson, Stolze, Hoffman, Wächter, Kmentt, Veasey, Kuen, Schwer,
    Equiluz, Gestner, Proebstl, Krause, Douglas, Koznowski, Holecek,
    Kirschbichler, Maikl
    VPO   10/61   SET 228/9   OSA 1218

Till Eulenspiegels lustige Streiche Op. 28
CSO 5/75 SXL 6749 CS 6978

STRAVINSKY, Igor
Oedipus Rex
Pears, Meyer, McIntyre, McCowen, Dean
JAC/LPO 3/76 SET 616 OSA 1168

Le Sacre du Printemps
CSO 5/74 SXL 6691 CS 6885

SUPPÉ, Franz von
Overtures: Light Cavalry, Poet and Peasant, Morning Noon and Night in
Vienna, Pique Dame
LPO 4/51 ACL 87 LL 352
VPO 5/59 SPA 374 CS 6779

TCHAIKOVSKY, Peter Ilich
Eugene Onegin Op. 24: Act I — Tatiana's Letter Scene
Tebaldi
CLOO c. 1956 LXT 5326 A 5320
: Complete
Kubiak, Hamari, Weikl, Burrows, Ghiaurov
JAC/ROHO 6-7/74 SET 596/8 OSA 13112

Piano Concerto No. 1 in B flat minor Op. 23
Curzon
VPO 10/58 SDD 191 CS 6100

Serenade for Strings Op. 48
IPO 11/58 SDD 205 STS 15141

Symphony No. 2 in C minor Op. 17
PCO 5/56 ECS 703 STS 15141

Symphony No. 5 in E minor Op. 64
PCO 5/56 SPA 223 STS 15060
CSO 5/75 SXL 6754 CS 6983

Symphony No. 6 in B minor Op. 74
CSO 5/76 SXL 6814 CS 7034

VERDI, Giuseppe
Aïda
Price, Vickers, Gorr, Merrill, Tozzi, Clabassi, Racciardi, Sighele
ROC/ROO 1961 SET 427/9 OSA 1393

Un Ballo in Maschera
Bergonzi, MacNeil, Nilsson, Simionato, Stahlman, Krause, Corena, Arbace,
de Palma
ASCC/ASCO 7/60 & 7/61 SET 215/7 OSA 1328

Don Carlos
Tebaldi, Bumbry, Bergonzi, Merrill, Ghiaurov, Talvela
ROHC/ROHO 64/65 SET 305/8 OSA 1432

Falstaff
Evans, Simionato, Ligabue, Merrill, Freni, Kraus
RCAC/RCAO 7/63 2BB 104/6 OSA 1395

La Forza de Destino: Overture
LPO   8/49   ACL 149   LL 200

Four Sacred Pieces
  Pickens
  CSC/CSO   5/77 & 5/78   SET 602   OS 26610

Otello
  M. Price, Cossutta, Bacquier, Dvorsky, Berbié, Moll, Equiluz, Dean, Helm
  VBC/VSOC/
  VPO   9/77   D102D 3   OSA 13130

Requiem
Sutherland, Horne, Pavarotti, Talvela
  VSOC/VPO   10/67   SET 374/5   OSA 1275
  Price, Baker, Luchetti, van Dam
  CSC/CSO   6/77   RL 22476   ARL 2 2476

Rigoletto
  Moffo, Merrill, Kraus, Elias, Flagello
  RCAC/RCAO   6/63   SER 5516/7   LSC 7027

La Traviata: Prelude to Acts 1 and 3
  ROHO   6/58   SPA 347   CS 6753

WAGNER, Richard
Der Fliegende Höllander: Overture
  VPO   10/61   SET 227   CS 6782
                 : **Complete**
  Bailey, Martin, Kollo, Talvela, Krenn
  CSC/CSO   5/76   D24D 3   OSA 13119

Götterdämmerung
  Nilsson, Ludwig, Neidlinger, Popp, Jones, Guy, Watts, Hoffman, Välkki,
  Windgassen, Frick, Fischer-Dieskau, Watson
  VSOC/VPO   5-6-10-11/64   SET 292/7   OSA 1604

Kinderkatechismus
  VPO   SET 406/8   RDNS 1

Die Meistersinger von Nürnberg: Prelude
  GSC/CSO   5/72   SXL 6684   CS 7078
                 : **Complete**
  Bailey, Moll, Kraus, Engel, Weikl, Nienstedt, Schomberg, Appel, Sénéchal,
  Berger-Tuna, Rydl, Hartmann, Kollo, Dallapozza, Bode, Hamari,
  Klumlikboldt
  VSOC/VPO   9-10/75   D13D 5   OSA 1512

Parsifal
  Kollo, Fischer-Dieskau, Hotter, Frick, Kélémen, Ludwig, Tear, Lackner,
  Hansliann, Schiml, Zednik, Aichberger, Popp, Hargan, Howells, te Kanawa,
  Knight, Lilowa, Finnilä
  VBC/VSOC/
  VPO   12/71-3/72   SET 550/4   OSA 1510

Das Rheingold
  London, Flagstad, Neidlinger, Svanholm, Wächter, Kmentt, Wohlfahrt,
  Kreppel, Böhme, Watson, Madeira, Balsborg, Plümacher, Malaniuk
  VPO   5-10/58   SET 242/6   OSA 1309

Rienzi: Overture
VPO   10/61   SET 227   CS 6782

Der Ring des Nibelungen: Complete
Singers and Choirs as listed under separate entries for each music drama
VPO   D100D 19   RINGS
            : An Introduction, with excerpts, narrated by
Deryck Cooke
Singers and Choirs as listed under separate entries for each music drama
VPO   SET 406/8   RDNS 1

Siegfried
Windgassen, Hotter, Nilsson, Stolze, Neidlinger, Böhme, Höffgen,
Sutherland
VPO   5-10/62   SET 242/6   OSA 1508

Siegfried Idyll
VPO   11/65   SET 323/4   CSA 2216

Tannhäuser: Overture and Venusberg Music
VPO   10/61   SET 227   CS 6782
            : Complete
Sotin, Kollo, Braun, Hollweg, Jungwirth, Equiluz, Bailey, Dernesch,
Ludwig
VBC/VPO   10/70   SET 506/9   OSA 1438
            : Overture
CSO   5/77   SXL 6856   CS 7078

Tristan und Isolde
Uhl, Nilsson, Resnik, van Mill, Krause, Kmentt, Klein, Kozub, Kirschbichler
VGM/VPO   9/60   SET 204/8   OSA 1502
            : Vorspiel and Liebestod
CSO   5/77   SXL 6856   CS 7078

Die Walküre: Act 2 — Todesverkundigung, and Act 3
Flagstad, Svanholm, Edelmann, Schech, Balsborg, Steingruber, Hoffman,
Bence, Watson, Rösler
VPO   5/57   GOS 577/8   OSA 1203
            : Complete
Nilsson, Hotter, Crespin, King, Ludwig, Frick, Schlosser, Fassbänder,
Lindholm, Tyler, Dernesch, Watts, Little, Hellman
VPO   10-11/65   SET 312/6   OSA 1509

WALTON, Sir William
Belshazzar's Feast,* Coronation Te Deum†
Luxon*
SCC†/WCC†/CCC†/
JAC*/LPO   3/77   SET 618   OS 26525

WEBER, Carl Maria von
Oberon Overture
CSO   11/73   SXL 6830   CS 7050

164

Selected Bibliography

Bloomfield, Arthur J., *The San Francisco Opera 1923-1961*. New York: Appleton-Century-Crofts, 1961.

Culshaw, John, *Ring Resounding*. New York: Viking, 1967.

Davis, Ronald, *Opera in Chicago*. New York: Appleton Century-Crofts, 1966.

Furlong, William Barry, *Season With Solti: A Year in the Life of the Chicago Symphony*. New York: Macmillan, 1974.

Haltrecht, Montague, *The Quiet Showman*. London: Collins, 1975.

Lawrence, Robert, *A Rage for Opera*. New York: Dodd, Mead, 1971.

Index

(of persons mentioned in the text)

SOLTI

"Solti is a 'shoo-in' for the World's Best Conductor title." *Alan Rich, New York Magazine*

Since becoming Music Director of the Chicago Symphony in 1969, Sir Georg Solti has often been the subject of such superlative statements. And no wonder. In addition to leading what many believe to be the finest orchestra of our time, Solti is the only conductor to have won the Grand Prix du Disque eleven times, the first conductor to produce a complete recording of Wagner's gigantic *Ring* cycle, and the single conductor generally credited for raising the standards of performance of Covent Garden to unprecedented heights.

Paul Robinson's book, in addition to giving details of Solti's life and career, is especially valuable for its detailed critical assessment of the recorded performances and includes chapters on Solti's Beethoven, Wagner and Mahler cycles.